The Creative Curriculum® *for* Preschool

Teaching Guide

featuring the Reduce, Reuse, Recycle Study

Kai-leé Berke, Carol Aghayan, Cate Heroman

TeachingStrategies® · Bethesda, MD

English editing: Lydia Paddock, Jayne Lytel
Design and layout: Jeff Cross, Amy Jackson, Abner Nieves
Spanish translation: Claudia Caicedo Núñez
Spanish editing: Judith F. Wohlberg, Alicia Fontán
Cover design: Laura Monger Design

Teaching Strategies, LLC
7101 Wisconsin Avenue, Suite 700
Bethesda, MD 20814

www.TeachingStrategies.com

978-1-60617-386-2

Library of Congress Cataloging-in-Publication Data

Berke, Kai-leé.
  The creative curriculum for preschool teaching guide featuring the reduce, reuse, recycle study / Kai-leé Berke, Carol Aghayan, Cate Heroman.
    p. cm.
  ISBN 978-1-60617-386-2
  1. Education, Preschool--Activity programs. 2. Recycling (Waste, etc.)--Study and teaching (Preschool)--Activity programs. I. Aghayan, Carol. II. Heroman, Cate. III. Title.
  LB1140.35.C74B46 2010
  372.1102--dc22
                    2010002625

Teaching Strategies and The Creative Curriculum names and logos are registered trademarks of Teaching Strategies, LLC, Bethesda, MD. This *Teaching Guide* is based on *The Creative Curriculum® Study Starters: Trash and Garbage* (Charlotte Stetson, lead author). Brand-name products of other companies are given for illustrative purposes only and are not required for implementation of the curriculum.

5 6 7 8 9 10 11 12   20 19 18 17 16 15 14
     Printing   Year Printed

Printed and bound in the United States of America

Acknowledgments

Many people helped with the creation of this *Teaching Guide* and the supporting teaching tools. We would like to thank Hilary Parrish Nelson for her guidance as our supportive Editorial Director and Jo Wilson for patiently keeping us on task. Both Hilary and Jan Greenberg provided a thoughtful and detailed content review that strengthened the final product.

Sherrie Rudick, Jan Greenberg, and Larry Bram deserve recognition for creating the first-ever children's book collection at Teaching Strategies, LLC. Working with Q2AMedia, they developed the concept for each book and saw the development process through from start to finish. Their hard work, creativity, patience, and attention to detail shines through in the finished product.

We are grateful to Dr. Lea McGee for her guidance, review, and feedback on our *Book Discussion Cards*. Jan Greenberg and Jessika Wellisch interpreted her research on a repeated read-aloud strategy to create a set of meaningful book discussion cards.

Thank you to Heather Baker, Toni Bickart, and Dr. Steve Sanders for writing more than 200 *Intentional Teaching Cards*, carefully aligning each teaching sequence with the related developmental progression and ensuring that children will receive the individualized instruction that they need to be successful learners. We are grateful to Sue Mistrett, who carefully reviewed each card and added strategies for including all children.

Translating *Mighty Minutes* into Spanish, ensuring cultural and linguistic appropriateness, was no easy task. Thank you to our dedicated team of writers and editors, including Spanish Educational Publishing, Dawn Terrill, Giuliana Rovedo, and Mary Conte.

Our brilliant editorial team, Toni Bickart, Lydia Paddock, Jayne Lytel, Diane Silver, Heather Schmitt, Heather Baker, Judy Wohlberg, Dawn Terrill, Giuliana Rovedo, Victory Productions, Elizabeth Tadlock, Reneé Fendrich, Kristyn Oldendorf, and Celine Tobal reviewed, refined, questioned, and sometimes rewrote our words, strengthening each page they touched.

Thank you to our Creative Services team for taking our words and putting them into a design that is both beautiful and easily accessible. The creative vision of Margot Ziperman, Abner Nieves, Jeff Cross, and Amy Jackson is deeply appreciated.

Our esteemed Latino Advisory Committee helped us continually reflect on how to support Spanish-speaking children and guided us through the development process. Thank you to Dr. Dina Castro, Dr. Linda Espinosa, Antonia Lopez, Dr. Lisa Lopez, and Dr. Patton Tabors.

We would like to acknowledge Lilian Katz and Sylvia Chard for their inspiring work on the Project Approach that has greatly advanced our thinking about quality curriculum for young children.

Most importantly, we would never be able to do this without the visionary guidance of Diane Trister Dodge. Her thoughtful leadership and commitment to young children and their families inspires all of the work that we do at Teaching Strategies.

Table of Contents

Getting Started

Why Investigate Reducing, Reusing, and Recycling?

Trash and garbage are all around us. We find rubbish and waste in our homes, on the streets, and in places where we work and play. We pay more attention to garbage when it becomes a problem: a community with more garbage than it can dispose of faces the prospect of a new landfill; dangerous waste begins to affect people's health; a tragedy, such as a hurricane, produces mountains of debris; or excessive litter creates an eyesore. However, once immediate problems are resolved, we often forget about the ongoing challenge of dealing with trash and garbage.

Children are fascinated by what is in garbage cans and often pick up trash against our wishes. This natural curiosity provides a good starting point for finding out what happens to trash after it's thrown away and exploring the concept of reducing, reusing, and recycling.

A study of reducing, reusing, and recycling not only offers opportunities for children to explore a topic that interests them but allows them to gather information, become more aware of the world around them, and solve problems. In this study, children will observe, gather data, explore their community, interview experts, learn new information, and propose solutions to problems. They will use skills in mathematics, literacy, the arts, and technology to represent their understanding of important concepts related to science and social studies.

> How do the children in your room show their interest in trash and garbage? How do they show their interest in what happens to garbage? What kinds of things do they say about it?

Web of Investigations

The *Teaching Guide Featuring the Reduce, Reuse, Recycle Study* includes five investigations aimed at exploring the concept of waste reduction. The investigations offer children an opportunity to learn more about trash and garbage, where it comes from, and why it can be a problem. Children will also learn to gather information to solve problems about reducing the amount of waste produced by society.

Some of the investigations also include site visits and classroom guest speakers. Each investigation helps children explore important concepts in science and social studies and strengthens their skills in literacy, math, technology, and the arts. Expand this web by adding your own ideas, particularly about aspects of the topic that are unique to your community.

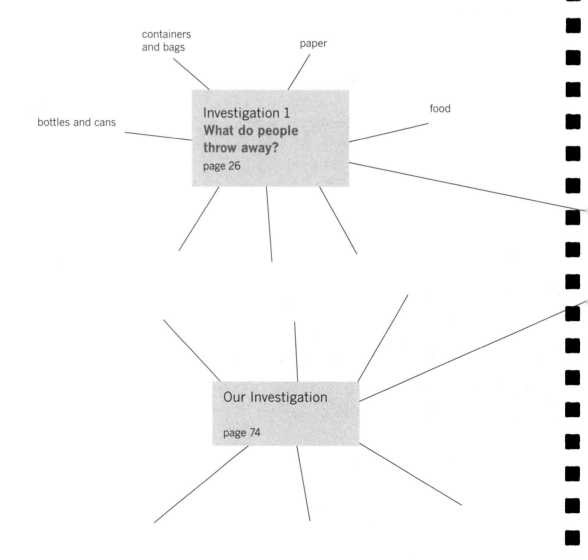

containers and bags

paper

bottles and cans

Investigation 1
What do people throw away?
page 26

food

Our Investigation

page 74

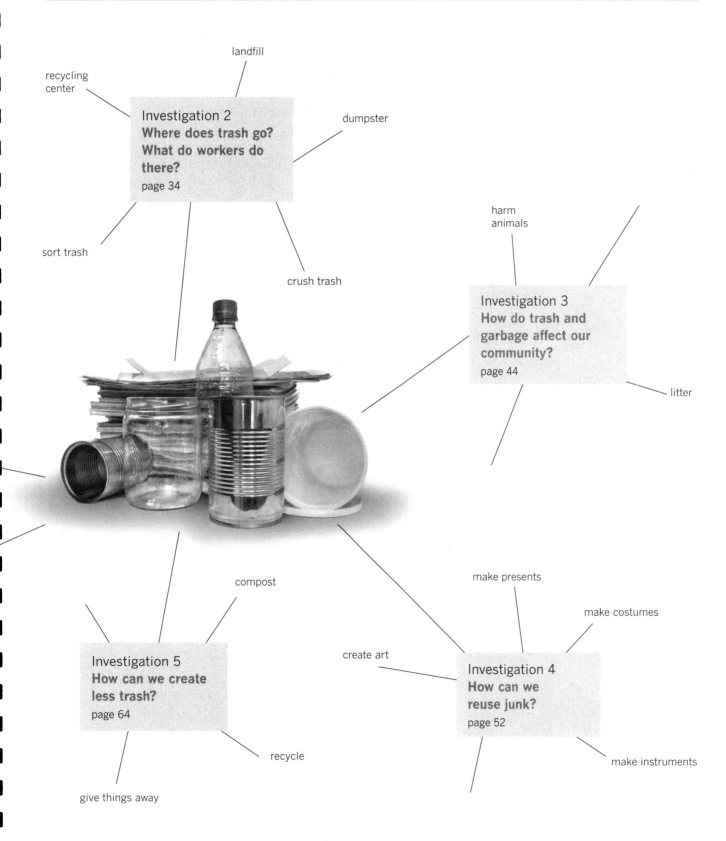

recycling
center

landfill

Investigation 2
**Where does trash go?
What do workers do
there?**
page 34

dumpster

sort trash

crush trash

harm
animals

Investigation 3
**How do trash and
garbage affect our
community?**
page 44

litter

compost

make presents

make costumes

create art

Investigation 5
**How can we create
less trash?**
page 64

Investigation 4
**How can we
reuse junk?**
page 52

recycle

make instruments

give things away

A Letter to Families

Send families a letter introducing the study. Use the letter to communicate with families and as an opportunity to invite their participation in the study.

Dear Families,

Most of us don't spend much time thinking about trash and garbage. We might give the problem some thought when our community needs a new landfill, a crisis about dangerous waste arises, or litter gets out of control. But then we often forget about the ever-present challenge of dealing with trash and garbage. We think studying how to reduce, reuse, and recycle trash and garbage will engage children because they are familiar with and curious about the topic.

We need your help gathering items to investigate. We'll need many different objects and pictures related to trash and garbage. We will begin our study by collecting them. Here's a list of suggested items, but you may also send in others not on the list as long as they are clean and safe.

Objects	Pictures
wastebaskets	litter-trash in various places
garbage-trash cans	dumps and landfills
recycling bins-boxes	garbage trucks
trash-garbage bags	street-cleaning vehicles
compost containers-bins	sanitation workers
paper shredder	recycling centers
clean and dry trash-junk items*	incinerators
can crushers	public trash receptacles

* paper towel rolls, empty plastic containers, cans with dull edges, empty packaging, fabric scraps, leftover wrapping paper, rinsed tinfoil, old telephones or radios without batteries, wood scraps, empty spools, rinsed milk cartons, old magazines, and bottle tops

As we study trash and garbage and how we can reduce, reuse, and recycle, we will learn concepts and skills in literacy, math, science, social studies, the arts, and technology. We will also be developing thinking skills to observe, investigate, ask questions, solve problems, make predictions, and test our ideas.

What You Can Do at Home

Talk with your child about trash and garbage. Help raise your child's awareness of the kinds of trash and garbage your family creates each day. If you dispose of your trash at a dump or landfill, take your child along to see where the trash goes. Borrow some library books about trash, garbage, and recycling. If you recycle at home, help your child take responsibility for sorting items into your family's recycling boxes.

When you are outside with your child and you notice a piece of trash on the ground, point it out and talk about it. For example, say, "I wonder why someone dropped that candy wrapper on the ground. Is it supposed to be there? Is there a better place to put it?"

At the end of the study, we will have a special event to show you what we've learned. Thank you for playing an important role in our learning.

Carta a las familias

Envíe una carta a las familias para informarles sobre el estudio. Use la carta para comunicarse y como una oportunidad para invitarles a participar.

Apreciadas familias,

La mayoría de nosotros no dedica mucho tiempo a pensar acerca de la basura. Es posible que pensemos en ello si en nuestra comunidad se necesita un nuevo relleno sanitario, si hay una crisis a causa de los desechos peligrosos o cuando la basura ya no es controlable. Pero a menudo olvidamos el continuo reto de ocuparnos de ella. Nosotros pensamos que estudiar el tema de cómo reducir, reutilizar y reciclar la basura les permitirá a los niños aprender debido a su familiaridad y curiosidad con respecto a este tema.

Para poder iniciar nuestro estudio nosotros necesitamos de su ayuda para reunir unos cuantos objetos. Para ello necesitaremos objetos e imágenes relacionadas con la basura. A continuación ofrecemos algunas sugerencias, pero siéntanse libres para enviar cualquier elemento que esté limpio y sea seguro.

Objetos	Imágenes
papeleras	basura en varios lugares
botes de basura	basureros o rellenos sanitarios
cajas o recipientes de reciclaje	camiones de basura
bolsas para la basura	vehículos de limpieza de calles
recipientes para abono orgánico	personas que trabajan en limpieza
trituradora de papel	centros de reciclaje
	incineradores
	recipientes públicos para la basura

objetos para desechar limpios y secos, p. ej., tubos de toallas de papel, recipientes de plástico vacíos, latas sin bordes afilados, empaques vacíos, pedazos de tela, pedazos de papel de envolver, papel de aluminio limpio, teléfonos o radios viejos sin pilas, pedazos de madera, carretes vacíos, cartones de leche lavados, revistas viejas y tapas de botellas.

A medida que estudiemos la basura, y cómo podemos reducir, reutilizar y reciclar, se aprenderán conceptos y se desarrollarán destrezas en lectoescritura, matemáticas, ciencia, estudios sociales, tecnología y las artes, al tiempo que se desarrollará el razonamiento investigando, haciendo preguntas, resolviendo problemas, haciendo predicciones y comprobando ideas.

Qué se puede hacer en el hogar

Hablen con los niños acerca de la basura. Ayúdenles a ser conscientes de la clase de basura que su familia produce diariamente. Si ustedes la desechan en un basurero o vertedero de basura, lleven al niño o niña para que vea a dónde se lleva la basura. Saquen algunos libros de la biblioteca que traten de la basura y el reciclaje. Si en su casa se recicla, ayuden a que el niño se encargue de separar las cosas en las distintas cajas de reciclaje.

Cuando salgan y noten un pedazo de papel en el suelo, señálenlo y hablen de ello. Diga, por ejemplo, "Me pregunto por qué alguien tiró ese papel en el suelo. ¿Crees que debe estar allí? ¿Hay un mejor lugar para colocarlo?"

Al finalizar nuestro estudio, tendremos un evento especial para celebrar lo aprendido. De antemano, les agradecemos su participación y su importante rol en nuestro aprendizaje.

Beginning the Study

Introducing the Topic

To begin this study, you will explore the topic with the children to answer the following questions: What do we know about reducing, reusing, and recycling? What do we want to find out about reducing, reusing, and recycling?

Begin gathering many different types of reusable junk and other trash-related items that you will use throughout the study. Ask the children, their families, and friends to help you build the collection. A sample letter to families is included in the beginning of this *Teaching Guide*.

Below are some suggestions for different kinds of items to gather.

To ensure children's safety, it is important that you carefully inspect all trash items brought into school. Check for sharp edges, cleanliness, and suitability for handling by young children.

Build on children's natural interest in trash as junk arrives in the classroom. Since children will be very curious about the junk collection, think about how to store and display the items so that children can easily see and examine them. Consider providing several clear bins for sorting the materials.

As the collection grows, start talking about individual items. Help children learn the names of the objects. Have them describe the items and talk about any previous experiences with them. Help children notice similarities and differences, make comparisons, and hypothesize about how the various items are (or were) used.

"How do you think this was used?"

"What do you notice about the materials used to make this?"

"Where have you seen some of these things before?"

"Who might use these things?"

"How do these things help people? How do they hurt people?"

> **What other open-ended questions, or prompts, can you use to stimulate discussion with children?**

Objects	Pictures
wastebaskets	litter (trash) in various places
garbage (trash) cans	dumps and landfills
recycling bins (boxes)	garbage trucks
trash (garbage) bags	street-cleaning vehicles
compost containers (bins)	sanitation workers
paper shredder	recycling centers
clean and dry trash (junk items*)	incinerators
can crushers	public trash receptacles

* paper towel rolls, empty plastic containers, cans with dull edges, empty packaging, fabric scraps, leftover wrapping paper, rinsed tinfoil, old telephones or radios without batteries, wood scraps, empty spools, rinsed milk cartons, old magazines, and bottle tops

Children's questions will help you decide what experiences to offer them and which investigations to pursue. During a group time, ask, "What should we try to find out about reducing, reusing, and recycling?" Record children's questions on a chart.

Model your own curiosity by wondering aloud, "I wonder how this trash got on our playground."

Verbalize questions that children may be thinking. Say, "It looks like you're trying to figure out how to use that paper towel roll to make something else. Let's add, 'How can we reuse the items in our junk collection?' to our list of questions."

Help younger children, or those with limited experience asking questions, formulate questions. If a child says, "My daddy gave away our old lawnmower," you could say, "Hmmm. Your daddy gave something to someone else instead of throwing it away. What other things could we give to someone else to use? I'll add that question to the chart so we can find out."

Preparing For Wow! Experiences

The "At a Glance" pages list these suggested Wow! Experiences, which require some advance planning.

Investigation 1:	Day 3: A walk around the school
Investigation 2:	Day 2: An interview with the school custodian and a tour of the path that trash takes through the school
	Day 3: An interview with a sanitation worker and a look at a trash truck (If possible, schedule a site visit to a landfill or recycling center, and interview the workers.)
Investigation 3:	Day 3: A litter walk around the school
Investigation 4:	Day 2: A visit from a family member
Celebrate Learning:	Day 2: Family members visit for the celebration

Exploring the Topic

What do we know about reducing, reusing, and recycling?

	Day 1	Day 2	Day 3
Interest Areas	Library: books about trash, garbage, and recycling	Discovery: junk collection	Discovery: junk collection
Question of the Day	Did you see any trash outside today? (Display trash items that you found around the school.)	Does this feel smooth or rough? (Display an interesting item from the junk collection.)	What could we do with this junk? (Display an interesting item from the junk collection.)
Large Group	Game: What's Inside the Box? **Discussion and Shared Writing:** Found Trash **Materials:** Mighty Minutes 31, "What's Inside the Box?"; small object; box; digital camera; trash items found around the school	Song: "Three Rowdy Children" **Discussion and Shared Writing:** What Is This Junk? **Materials:** Mighty Minutes 53, "Three Rowdy Children"; basket; items from the junk collection	Song: "Clap a Friend's Name" **Discussion and Shared Writing:** What Do We Know About Reducing, Reusing, and Recycling? **Materials:** Mighty Minutes 40, "Clap a Friend's Name"; chart labeled, "What do we know about reducing, reusing, and recycling?"; junk collection; several empty plastic bottles
Read-Aloud	*The Paper Bag Princess* Book Discussion Card 08 (first read-aloud)	*Hush! A Thai Lullaby*	*The Paper Bag Princess* Book Discussion Card 08 (second read-aloud)
Small Group	Option 1: Letters, Letters, Letters Intentional Teaching Card LL07, "Letters, Letters, Letters"; alphabet rubber stamps; colored inkpads; construction paper **Option 2: Buried Treasures** Intentional Teaching Card LL21, "Buried Treasures"; magnetic letters; a large magnet; ruler; tape; sand table with sand	Option 1: Environmental Print Intentional Teaching Card LL23, "Playing With Environmental Print"; variety of environmental print **Option 2: Baggie Books** Intentional Teaching Card LL20, "Baggie Books"; 6–8 resealable bags per book; environmental print; construction paper; scissors; stapler; colorful tape	Option 1: Junk Collage Intentional Teaching Card LL32, "Describing Art"; junk collection; paper; markers; scissors; glue **Option 2: Junk Sculpture** Intentional Teaching Card LL32, "Describing Art"; junk collection; scissors; glue; tape; modeling clay
Mighty Minutes™	Mighty Minutes 21, "Hully Gully, How Many?"; assorted small objects, e.g., coins, marbles, or bells	Mighty Minutes 21, "Hully Gully, How Many?"; assorted small objects, e.g., coins, marbles, or bells	Mighty Minutes 07, "Hippity, Hoppity, How Many?"

What do we want to find out?

Day 4	Day 5	Make Time For...
Discovery: junk collection **Art:** collage materials, e.g., paper scraps; tinfoil bits; old magazines and newspapers; cardboard pieces	**Art:** collage materials e.g., paper scraps; tinfoil bits; old magazines and newspapers; cardboard pieces	**Outdoor Experiences** **Physical Fun** • Review Intentional Teaching Card P19, "Bounce & Catch." Follow the guidance on the card.
What could we do with this junk? (Display an interesting item from the junk collection.)	Which game would you rather play: Simon Says or Jack in the Box?	**Family Partnerships** • Ask families to contribute to the collection by bringing in junk from home—items that typically get thrown away, e.g., paper towel rolls, old magazines, bottle tops, cartons, broken things. Check all items and make sure they're safe; rinse containers and remove items with sharp edges.
Game: What's Inside the Box? **Discussion and Shared Writing:** What Do We Know About Reducing, Reusing, and Recycling? **Materials:** Mighty Minutes 31, "What's Inside the Box?"; small object from home that ordinarily gets thrown away; box; basket; junk collection; paper towel roll; tape	**Game:** Simon Says or Jack in the Box **Discussion and Shared Writing:** What Do We Want to Find Out About Reducing, Reusing, and Recycling? **Materials:** Mighty Minutes 13, "Simon Says"; Mighty Minutes 74, "Jack in the Box"; *Dinosaur Woods*	• Set aside any boxes and packaging with clearly visible environmental print, e.g., letters, numbers, and shapes found in logos for products and stores.
Hush! A Thai Lullaby	*The Paper Bag Princess* Book Discussion Card 08 (third read-aloud)	
Option 1: Bounce & Count Intentional Teaching Card M18, "Bounce & Count"; variety of balls **Option 2: Junk Numbers** Intentional Teaching Card M04, "Number Cards"; junk collection; set of cards with a numeral and its number word printed on one side	**Option 1: Tallying the Junk** Intentional Teaching Card M06, "Tallying"; clipboard; paper; pencils or crayons; junk collection **Option 2: How Many Kinds?** Intentional Teaching Card M02, "Counting & Comparing"; card stock; marker; junk collection	
Mighty Minutes 72, "My Body Jumps"	Mighty Minutes 24, "Dinky Doo"	

Exploring the Topic

What do we know about reducing, reusing, and recycling?

What do we want to find out?

Vocabulary

English: *recycling*

Spanish: *reciclaje*

See Book Discussion Card 08, *The Paper Bag Princess*
(*La princesa vestida con una bolsa de papel*), for additional words.

Large Group

Opening Routine

- Sing a welcome song and talk about who's here.

> See *Beginning the Year* for more information and ideas about planning your opening routine. See Intentional Teaching Card SE02, "Look Who's Here!" for attendance chart ideas.

Game: What's Inside the Box?

- Use Mighty Minutes 31, "What's Inside the Box?"

- Follow the guidance on the card. Use something interesting that you would otherwise throw away, e.g., an empty egg carton, a plastic container, or fabric scrap.

> Use your best judgment about the kinds of trash items that you allow into the classroom. Pay extra attention to how you instruct children to handle them.

Discussion and Shared Writing: Found Trash

- Take a walk around the school before children arrive. Pay attention to any trash you see on the school grounds. Photograph or collect some of it.

- Show the trash, or photos, from your morning walk.

- Explain, "I was walking around our school this morning, and I found this."

- Ask, "What is it? How do you think it got there? Who do you think might have used it?"

- Record children's responses.

- Review the question of the day located on the "At a Glance" chart. Invite children to talk about the trash they saw.

English-language learners

Remember, some open-ended questions may be too difficult for beginning English-language learners to answer. If that is the case, ask closed questions, e.g., "Did it fall out of someone's pocket? Did someone throw it on the ground?" As you ask questions, use gestures to help children understand, e.g., toss something to the floor.

Before transitioning to interest areas, describe the books about trash, garbage, and recycling in the Library area. As you display individual books, build children's interest in the books by pointing out pictures and information.

Choice Time	As you interact with children in the interest areas, make time to • Explore the new books in the Library area with the children. • Explain new vocabulary, e.g., *recycling*.	• Pay attention to what children know, what they find interesting, and what questions they ask. Record their ideas.

Read-Aloud	Read *The Paper Bag Princess.* • Use Book Discussion Card 08, *The Paper Bag Princess.* Follow the guidance for the first read-aloud.

Small Group	**Option 1: Letters, Letters, Letters** • Review Intentional Teaching Card LL07, "Letters, Letters, Letters." Follow the guidance on the card.	**Option 2: Buried Treasures** • Review Intentional Teaching Card LL21, "Buried Treasures." Follow the guidance on the card.

Mighty Minutes™	• Use Mighty Minutes 21, "Hully Gully, How Many?" Follow the guidance on the card.

Large-Group Roundup	• Recall the day's events.	• Invite children who explored books about trash, garbage, and recycling in the Library area to share their discoveries.

Exploring the Topic

What do we know about reducing, reusing, and recycling?

What do we want to find out?

Vocabulary

English: *describe*
Spanish: *describir*

Large Group

Opening Routine

- Sing a welcome song and talk about who's here.

Song: "Three Rowdy Children"

- Use Mighty Minutes 53, "Three Rowdy Children." Follow the guidance on the card.

Discussion and Shared Writing: What Is This Junk?

- Pass around a basket of items from the junk collection.

- Invite children to select something that interests them.

- Ask, "Can you *describe* your object? How does your object look and feel?"

- Record children's descriptions.

- Expand on what children say by adding rich vocabulary, e.g., say, "Rohan said the tube he picked is scratchy. It does feel rough on my fingers when I touch it."

- Talk about the question of the day.

English-language learners
It is common for children to stop speaking their home language(s) and become temporarily nonverbal when they realize that others in class don't understand what they say. This does not indicate ability or unwillingness to participate in activities and discussions. Watch for nonverbal cues that signal a desire to participate, such as facial expressions, gestures, and other body movements,

---

Before transitioning to interest areas, talk about the growing junk collection in the Discovery area and how children may explore it.

Choice Time

As you interact with children in the interest areas, make time to

- Observe children as they explore the junk collection.

- Ask, "How might some of these things have been used?"

- Listen for what children already know about the study topic.

Read-Aloud

Read *Hush! A Thai Lullaby*.

- **Before you read**, ask, "What do you think this book will be about?"

- **As you read**, use your voice in different ways to reflect the tone of the book, e.g., a mother's soothing voice; big, loud animal sounds; and little, soft animal sounds.

- **After you read**, ask, "Why didn't the baby fall asleep?"

English-language learners
Changing the way you speak, e.g., adjusting volume, pitch, and rate, can aid children's comprehension.

Small Group

Option 1: Environmental Print

- Review Intentional Teaching Card LL23, "Playing With Environmental Print." Follow the guidance on the card.

Option 2: Baggie Books

- Review Intentional Teaching Card LL20, "Baggie Books." Follow the guidance on the card.

As you continue to build the classroom junk collection, make sure to include items with print, such as boxes, bags, old clothing, and bottles with labels. Children often first recognize these words by sight. Environmental print helps them understand that reading is finding out the meaning of text and not just sounding out words.

Mighty Minutes™

Use Mighty Minutes 21, "Hully Gully, How Many?" Try the variation on the back of the card.

Large-Group Roundup

- Recall the day's events.

- Invite children who explored the junk collection in the Discovery area to share their observations about an interesting piece of junk.

What do we know about reducing, reusing, and recycling?

What do we want to find out?

Vocabulary

English: *reuse, reduce, organize*

Spanish: *reutilizar, reducir, organizar*

See Book Discussion Card 08, *The Paper Bag Princess (La princesa vestida con una bolsa de papel)*, for additional words.

Large Group

Opening Routine

- Sing a welcome song and talk about who's here.

Song: "Clap a Friend's Name"

- Use Mighty Minutes 40, "Clap a Friend's Name." Follow the guidance on the card.

Discussion and Shared Writing: What Do We Know About Reducing, Reusing, and Recycling?

- Use the growing junk collection, as well as other items, to help children think about what they already know about reducing, reusing, and recycling.

- Show an empty plastic bottle. Ask, "What should I do with this bottle? How could I *reuse* it—use it again?"

- Record children's ideas on a chart labeled, "What we know about reducing, reusing, and recycling."

- Now show several empty plastic bottles. Say, "We have a lot of plastic bottles. How might we reduce the number of bottles we use? How might we use fewer bottles?"

- Record children's ideas on the chart.

Before transitioning to interest areas, talk about the growing collection of junk in the Discovery area. Explain, "I need you to help me to think of a way to *organize* the junk collection today during choice time."

Choice Time

As you interact with children in the interest areas, make time to

- Ask, "What different kinds of junk do we have?"

- Ask, "How can we organize these items?" If children need help, ask, "How are some of the items the same? How are they different?"

- Invite children to sort the junk into categories.

Read-Aloud

Read *The Paper Bag Princess.*

- Use Book Discussion Card 08, *The Paper Bag Princess*. Follow the guidance for the second read-aloud.

Small Group

Option 1: Junk Collage

- Review Intentional Teaching Card LL32, "Describing Art." Follow the guidance on the card.

- Give children various items from the junk collection along with paper, markers, scissors, and glue. Invite them to create a collage.

Option 2: Junk Sculpture

- Review Intentional Teaching Card LL32, "Describing Art." Follow the guidance on the card.

- Give children various items from the junk collection along with glue, tape, scissors, and modeling clay. Invite them to create a sculpture.

> See *The Creative Curriculum for Preschool, Volume 2: Interest Areas,* Chapter 9, "Art" for more information on how art promotes children's development and learning.

Mighty Minutes™

- Use Mighty Minutes 7, "Hippity, Hoppity, How Many?" Follow the guidance on the card.

Large-Group Roundup

- Recall the day's events.

- Review the question of the day.

- Invite children to share the collages or sculptures they created during small-group time.

Day 4　Exploring the Topic

What do we know about reducing, reusing, and recycling?

What do we want to find out?

Vocabulary

English: *reuse, recycling, organize*

Spanish: *reutilizar, reducir, organizar*

Large Group

Opening Routine

- Sing a welcome song and talk about who's here.

Game: What's Inside the Box?

- Use Mighty Minutes 31, "What's Inside the Box?" Follow the guidance on the card.

- Use a small object from home that ordinarily gets thrown away.

Discussion and Shared Writing: What Do We Know About Reducing, Reusing, and Recycling?

- Pass around another basket of items from the junk collection.

- Point out some items that would be thrown away and some that could be recycled.

- Ask, "What do you know about *recycling*?"

- Cut a paper towel roll in half, and tape the two rolls together to create a pair of pretend binoculars. Look through them, and explain, "Sometimes we can use things that we might throw away to make something new."

- Ask, "Did anyone find anything in the basket that could be used in a new way?"

- Talk about the question of the day.

- Record children's ideas on the chart labeled, "What we know about reducing, reusing, and recycling."

Before transitioning to interest areas, talk about the collage materials in the Art area. Also talk about the junk collection in the Discovery area, and tell the children that they may continue to organize the items. Invite children who sorted junk yesterday to share what they did.

> Helping children link what they already know with new information is likely to improve their comprehension and ability to remember the new content.

Choice Time

As you interact with children in the interest areas, make time to

- Invite children to think of a way to organize the junk collection and display the items in categories.

- Have children help make signs to label the categories.

- Talk with children about their work in the Art area.

English-language learners
Consider making category signs in all of the languages spoken in your class. This will make the children feel welcome, help them think about the categories, and promote literacy. You may also wish to color code the languages, e.g., blue labels for English and red for Spanish. If you take this approach, keep the coding system consistent throughout the classroom.

Read-Aloud

Read *Hush! A Thai Lullaby.*

- **Before you read**, ask, "What is this story about?"

- **As you read**, invite children to find the baby in the illustrations.

- **After you read**, look through the illustrations with the children. Talk about the illustrator's use of collage.

Small Group

Option 1: Bounce & Count

- Review Intentional Teaching Card M18, "Bounce & Count." Follow the guidance on the card.

Option 2: Junk Numbers

- Review Intentional Teaching Card M04, "Number Cards." Follow the guidance on the card using the junk collection.

Mighty Minutes™

- Use Mighty Minutes 72, "My Body Jumps." Try the rhyming variation on the back of the card.

Large-Group Roundup

- Recall the day's events.

- Invite children who organized the junk collection in the Discovery area to talk about how they grouped the junk.

What do we know about reducing, reusing, and recycling?

What do we want to find out?

Vocabulary

See Book Discussion Card 08, *The Paper Bag Princess (La princesa vestida con una bolsa de papel)*, for words.

Large Group

Opening Routine

- Sing a welcome song and talk about who's here.

Game: Simon Says or Jack in the Box

- Review Mighty Minutes 13, "Simon Says" and Mighty Minutes 74, "Jack in the Box."

- Talk about the question of the day. Make sure each child has cast a vote for the game that he or she would like to play.

- Discuss the voting results.

- Follow the guidance on the card for the most popular game.

**Discussion and Shared Writing:
What Do We Want to Find Out About
Reducing, Reusing, and Recycling?**

- Post the "What we know about reducing, reusing, and recycling" chart near the group area so you can refer to it often.

- Say, "We already know a lot of things about reducing, reusing, and recycling. Now let's think about what we want to find out about them."

- Model the questioning process for children. For example, show the children a recycling bin and wonder aloud about what you should put in it: "Hmmm, what should I put in this recycling bin?"

- Record children's questions.

- Help children formulate questions and expand their language. For example, a child says, "Mr. Finn takes our trash away. Maybe he takes it all home." You might say, "You're thinking about where Mr. Finn takes our trash when he empties our trash cans each day. I'll write the question, 'Where does Mr. Finn take our classroom trash?' on the chart.'"

> **More questions will emerge during investigations. Help children learn the meaning of the word *question*. For example, say, "That's a good *question*, Gina. Let's write it on our chart, and we'll try to find out the answer."**

Before transitioning to interest areas, read *Dinosaur Woods* with the children. Point out the collage style of art that was used to illustrate the story. After reading, talk about the collage materials in the Art area and how children may use them.

Choice Time

As you interact with children in the interest areas, make time to

- Talk with them about their artwork and the process they used to create it. Write down what they say.

- Display children's descriptions next to their artwork.

Read-Aloud

Read *The Paper Bag Princess.*

- Use Book Discussion Card 08, *The Paper Bag Princess.* Follow the guidance for the third read-aloud.

Small Group

Option 1: Tallying the Junk

- Review Intentional Teaching Card M06, "Tallying." Follow the guidance on the card using the junk collection.

Option 2: How Many Kinds?

- Review Intentional Teaching Card M02, "Counting & Comparing." Follow the guidance on the card using the junk collection.

> **Learning to tally helps children understand one-to-one correspondence, an important skill related to number concepts.**

Mighty Minutes™

- Use Mighty Minutes 24, "Dinky Doo." Follow the guidance on the card.

Large-Group Roundup

- Recall the day's events.

- Invite children who made collages in the Art area to share their work.

Investigating the Topic

Introduction

You have already started lists of children's ideas and questions about reducing, reusing, and recycling. As you implement the study, you will design investigations that help the children expand their ideas, find answers to their questions, and learn important skills and concepts. This section has daily plans for investigating questions that children ask. Do not be limited by these suggestions. Use them as inspiration to design experiences tailored to your own group of children and the resources in your school and community. While it is important to respond to children's ideas and follow their lead as their thinking evolves, it is also important for you to organize the study and plan for possibilities.

Investigation 1

What do people throw away?

	Day 1	Day 2
Interest Areas	**Discovery:** junk collection; poster board, cardboard, or heavy paper; glue	**Library:** environmental print from the junk collection
Question of the Day	What did you throw away today?	Does all trash stink?
Large Group	**Movement:** Let's Stick Together **Discussion and Shared Writing:** Classroom Trash **Materials:** Mighty Minutes 67, "Let's Stick Together"; select bag of trash with items such as a worn-out marker, crumpled paper, damp paper towel, empty container, crayon box; gloves	**Movement:** Bouncing Big Brown Balls **Discussion and Shared Writing:** Trash and Garbage at Home **Materials:** Mighty Minutes 43, "Bouncing Big Brown Balls"; photos or drawings that children brought; piece of trash with familiar environmental print; photo of your home trash can
Read-Aloud	*Something From Nothing*	*I Stink!*
Small Group	**Option 1: Story Problems** Intentional Teaching Card M22, "Story Problems"; collection of manipulatives **Option 2: Bowling Math** Intentional Teaching Card M22, "Story Problems"; 10 plastic bottles partially filled with sand or small rocks; soft ball	**Option 1: Junk Patterns** Intentional Teaching Card M14, "Patterns"; junk collection; construction paper; crayons or markers **Option 2: Action Patterns** Intentional Teaching Card M35, "Action Patterns"; action cards; pocket chart
Mighty Minutes™	Mighty Minutes 68, "I Have a Secret"; yarn or hula hoops; various objects to sort	Mighty Minutes 36, "Body Patterns"

Day 3	Make Time For...

Toys and Games: bowling pins made from plastic bottles partially filled with sand or rocks; soft ball

Where will we find a trash can on our walk today? (Display a picture of two places in the school.)

Game: Body Patterns

Discussion and Shared Writing: What Do People Throw Away Around the School?

Materials: Mighty Minutes 36, "Body Patterns"; Intentional Teaching Card SE01, "Site Visits"; small clipboards; paper and pencils

Radio Man
Book Discussion Card 11
(first read-aloud)

Option 1: Alphabet Cards

Intentional Teaching Card LL03, "Alphabet Cards"; letter cards; small manipulatives; junk collection

Option 2: Textured Letters

Intentional Teaching Card LL15, "Textured Letters"; junk collection; heavy paper or card stock; letter made out of a variety of materials

Mighty Minutes 65, "People Patterns"

Outdoor Experiences

- Bury outdoors a piece of organic garbage, such as an apple core or a banana peel. Pay attention to where you bury it because you'll be digging it up later in the study when talking about composting.

Physical Fun

- Review Intentional Teaching Card P20, "Body Shapes & Sizes." Follow the guidance on the card.

Family Partnerships

- Send a note home to families asking them to discuss with their children what things the family typically throws away. Explain in the note that you've asked children to bring in various kinds of trash, such as an empty carton or leftover wrapping paper, that can be used to create something useful.

Wow! Experiences

- Day 3: A walk around the school to investigate trash cans in different areas, e.g., the kitchen, classroom, and office

Investigation 1

What do people throw away?

Vocabulary

English: *something, nothing*

Spanish: *algo, nada*

Large Group

Opening Routine

- Sing a welcome song and talk about who's here.

Movement: Let's Stick Together

- Use Mighty Minutes 67, "Let's Stick Together." Follow the guidance on the card.

Discussion and Shared Writing: Classroom Trash

- Review the question of the day.

- Gather a bag of selected classroom trash.

> When collecting classroom trash, include items that would ordinarily be thrown away in the classroom. Do not include food or hazardous items.

- Show the children the bag of trash. Explain, "This is a bag of trash from our classroom. I wonder what will be in it."

- Invite the children to predict what will be in the bag. Record their predictions.

- Put on a pair of gloves. Explain that it's important to wear gloves when exploring trash because of the germs in it. If possible, give children gloves so that they can pull items out of the bag.

- Examine the bag of trash, and talk about what people are throwing away in the classroom.

- Make a list of the items in the bag. Label the chart, "What's in our classroom trash?"

- Ask, "What would be in our trash after snack time?" Record the children's responses on the chart.

Before transitioning to interest areas, invite children to help you sort the trash in the Discovery area.

Choice Time

As you interact with children in the interest areas, make time to

- Ask, "What are the different types of trash in the classroom trash bag?"

- Wonder aloud about the materials, and pose questions to help children sort the objects, e.g., "Hmmm... this cup is plastic. This marker's cap is plastic. Is there any other plastic trash?"

- Invite children to sort the trash onto three different pieces of posterboard, cardboard, or heavy paper, using one piece each for plastic, metal, and paper.

- Have the children glue the sorted items onto the paper to make a display.

Read-Aloud

Read *Something From Nothing.*

- **Before you read**, tell children the name of the book. Say, "I wonder how you can make *something* from *nothing.*"

- **As you read**, pause and invite predictions about what the grandfather will make.

- **After you read**, ask, "How did he make *something* from *nothing?*"

Small Group

Option 1: Story Problems

- Review Intentional Teaching Card M22, "Story Problems." Follow the guidance on the card.

Option 2: Bowling Math

- Review Intentional Teaching Card M22, "Story Problems."

- Create a bowling game. Make 10 bowling pins out of empty plastic bottles partially filled with sand. Use a soft ball.

- Invite the children to play the bowling game with you. Give them a few minutes to play with the materials.

- Then follow the guidance on the card to create story problems using the bowling game materials.

> **Bowling is a fun way to learn subtraction skills and how to separate, or decompose, numbers. Children will learn basic subtraction skills and different ways to make a group of 10 items.**

Mighty Minutes™

- Use Mighty Minutes 68, "I Have a Secret."

- Follow the guidance on the card using items from the junk collection.

Large-Group Roundup

- Recall the day's events.

- Invite children who created trash displays to share their work.

- Help children think of questions to ask their families about the trash at home. Record their questions on chart paper and hang it for families to see when they pick up their children.

- Remind children to interview their family about what they throw away. Invite them to draw or photograph the contents of the family trash can.

> **For families who don't pick up their children from school, themselves, try generating these questions earlier in the day. Copy them for children to take home.**

Day 2 Investigation 1

What do people throw away?

Vocabulary

English: *compacted*

Spanish: *compactado*

Large Group

Opening Routine

- Sing a welcome song and talk about who's here.

Movement: Bouncing Big Brown Balls

- Use Mighty Minutes 43, "Bouncing Big Brown Balls."

- Try the trash and garbage version on the back of the card, and add other lines, e.g., "We're picking up the trash."

Discussion and Shared Writing: Trash and Garbage at Home

- Show a photo of your trash can at home, and talk about what's in it.

- Ask children to recall their interviews with family members about what they throw away at home. Share any photos or drawings that the children brought in.

- Record their ideas on a chart labeled, "What's in our trash at home?"

- Talk about the differences between trash thrown away in the classroom and at home.

To create a word wall, display the letters of the alphabet at children's eye level. Under each letter add words (with pictures when possible) that begin with that letter. Begin your word wall with the names and photos of children in the classroom. Add words regularly throughout the year that are meaningful and familiar to the children, including study-related words. Encourage children to reference the word wall when they are writing.

Before transitioning to interest areas, show children a piece of your home trash with familiar print on it. Read the print aloud. Explain that children may help create (or add to) a word wall in the Library area with words found on items in the junk collection.

Choice Time

As you interact with children in the interest areas, make time to

- Help children identify and sort the environmental print.

- Talk about letters and invite children to read familiar words, e.g., say, "Marcus, this box has a bowl of cereal on the front. This word tells us what kind it is. That's right, it says, *Kix*®! *Kix*® starts with the letter *k*. That's the same letter that starts Kira's name. Do you see anything on these two boxes that starts with a *k*?"

English-language learners
Include items with environmental print in children's home languages. When possible, ask the families of English-language learners to contribute such items. Having environmental print in home languages helps all children participate and feel proud of their culture and families.

Read-Aloud

Read *I Stink!*

- **Before you read**, tell the children the title of the book. Ask, "What do you think this book is about?"

- **As you read**, inflect your voice to enliven your reading. Explain that you sometimes change your voice when the font changes. Define the word *compacted*.

- **After you read**, look back at the pages that show the different kinds of things people throw away. Discuss those items with the children.

- Review the question of the day.

Small Group

Option 1: Junk Patterns

- Review Intentional Teaching Card M14, "Patterns." Follow the guidance on the card using the junk collection.

Option 2: Action Patterns

- Review Intentional Teaching Card M35, "Action Patterns." Follow the guidance on the card.

Mighty Minutes™

- Use Mighty Minutes 36, "Body Patterns." Follow the guidance on the card.

Large-Group Roundup

- Recall the day's events.

- Invite children who helped create the word wall in the Library area to read the words on the display.

What do people throw away?

Vocabulary

See Book Discussion Card 11, *Radio Man* (*Don Radio*), for words.

Large Group

Opening Routine

- Sing a welcome song and talk about who's here.

Game: Body Patterns

- Use Mighty Minutes 36, "Body Patterns." Follow the guidance on the card.

Discussion and Shared Writing: What Do People Throw Away Around the School?

- Explain, "Today we will walk around the school and look in trash cans."

- Ask, "What do you think we'll find when we investigate the trash cans around the school? Do you think the trash will be different in different places?"

- Talk about how children may use their senses to learn more about the trash.

- Ask, "Why isn't it safe for us to touch the trash with our bare hands?" Talk about germs.

- Talk about the question of the day.

> **For more information about helping children record their discoveries on site visits, see Intentional Teaching Card LL45, "Observational Drawing."**

Before transitioning to interest areas, talk about the bowling game in the Toys and Games area and how children may use it.

Choice Time

As you interact with children in the interest areas, make time to

- Listen to children as they play the bowling game. Pay attention to their informal use of number words and concepts.

- Invite the children to count the bottles they knock over and the bottles left standing.

- Point out the shape that emerges when you set up the bowling pins (one pin in the first row, two pins in the second, three in the third, and four in the fourth).

English-language learners

Invite English-language learners to count in their home language(s) and in English. They may want to teach other children to count in their language(s).

Read-Aloud	Read *Radio Man.*
	• Use Book Discussion Card 11, *Radio Man.* Follow the guidance for the first read-aloud.

Small Group	**Option 1: Alphabet Cards**	**Option 2: Textured Letters**
	• Review Intentional Teaching Card LL03, "Alphabet Cards." Follow the guidance on the card using the junk collection.	• Review Intentional Teaching Card LL15, "Textured Letters." Follow the guidance on the card.
		• Create textured letter cards out of interesting materials from the junk collection.

Mighty Minutes™	• Use Mighty Minutes 65, "People Patterns." Follow the guidance on the card.

Large-Group Roundup	• Recall the day's events.
	• Invite children to share the observational drawings that they created on their walk around the school today.

Investigation 2

Where does trash go? What do workers do there?

	Day 1	Day 2	Day 3
Interest Areas	**Computer:** computer with Internet access; eBook version of *Sam Helps Recycle* Intentional Teaching Card LL26, "Searching the Web"	**Discovery:** items to take apart, e.g., old telephones and radios (remove batteries); screwdrivers	**Blocks:** garbage trucks **Computer:** computer with Internet access; eBook version of *Sam Helps Recycle*
Question of the Day	Where does our trash go after we throw it away?	Do you have a question for our visitor?	Do you have a question for our visitor?
Large Group	**Movement:** Going on a Journey **Discussion and Shared Writing:** Where Does the Trash Go? **Materials:** Mighty Minutes 63, "Going on a Journey"; paper, pencils, or markers; small clipboards	**Movement:** The Kids Go Marching In **Discussion and Shared Writing:** Follow That Trash **Materials:** Mighty Minutes 70, "The Kids Go Marching In"; map of school (can be teacher-created)	**Song:** "Recycle Song" **Discussion and Shared Writing:** Expert Interview **Materials:** Mighty Minutes 71, "Recycle Song"; recyclable cans and bottles; digital camera
Read-Aloud	*Sam Helps Recycle*	*Radio Man* Book Discussion Card 11 (second read-aloud)	*Sam Helps Recycle*
Small Group	**Option 1: Rhyming Riddles** Intentional Teaching Card LL11, "Rhyming Riddles"; props that rhyme **Option 2: Rhyming Chart** Intentional Teaching Card LL10, "Rhyming Chart"; poem or song with rhyming words; props that illustrate the poem or song	**Option 1: How Big Around?** Intentional Teaching Card M62, "How Big Around?"; variety of spherical objects; ball of yarn or string; scissors **Option 2: Which Container Holds More?** Intentional Teaching Card M32, "Which Container Holds More?"; sand table; various clear plastic containers; paper cup, measuring cup, or can; funnel	**Option 1: Bookmaking** Intentional Teaching Card LL04, "Bookmaking"; cardboard or card stock; blank paper; pencils, crayons, or markers; bookbinding supplies **Option 2: Desktop Publishing** Intentional Teaching Card LL02, "Desktop Publishing"
Mighty Minutes™	Mighty Minutes 72, "My Body Jumps"	Mighty Minutes 47, "Step Up"	Mighty Minutes 38, "Spatial Patterns"

Day 4	Make Time For...

Discovery: can crusher; empty cans; two identical small trash cans or other identical containers

Which has more cans? (Display two containers: one with crushed cans and one with uncrushed cans.)

Song: "Recycle Song"

Discussion and Shared Writing: Dump or Recycle?

Materials: Mighty Minutes 71, "Recycle Song"; recyclable cans and bottles; *Sam Helps Recycle*; select trash collection with recyclable and nonrecyclable items

Radio Man
Book Discussion Card 11
(third read-aloud)

Option 1: Bookmaking

Intentional Teaching Card LL04, "Bookmaking"; cardboard or card stock; blank paper; pencils, crayons, or markers; bookbinding supplies

Option 2: Desktop Publishing

Intentional Teaching Card LL02, "Desktop Publishing"; digital camera; computer; each child's word bank; printer; paper; bookbinding supplies

Mighty Minutes 01, "The People in Your Neighborhood"

Outdoor Experiences

Physical Fun

- Review Intentional Teaching Card P20, "Body Shapes & Sizes." Follow the guidance on the card.

Family Partnerships

- Ask families to bring in a piece of trash that has the recycling symbol on it.
- Invite families to access the eBook, *Sam Helps Recycle*.

Wow! Experiences

- Day 2: An interview with the school custodian and a tour of the path that the trash takes through the school
- Day 3: An interview with a sanitation worker and a look at a trash or recycling truck

Day 1   Investigation 2

Where does trash go?
What do workers do there?

Vocabulary

English: *recycle*

Spanish: *reciclar, reciclaje*

Large Group

Opening Routine

- Sing a welcome song and talk about who's here.

Movement: Going on a Journey

- Use Mighty Minutes 63, "Going on a Journey." Follow the guidance on the card.

Discussion and Shared Writing: Where Does the Trash Go?

- Talk about the question of the day.

- Say, "I wonder what happens to the trash after we put it in the trash can. Where do you think it goes? How can we find out?"

- Record children's responses.

- Invite children to draw a picture about where they think the trash goes. Record their ideas about where they think the trash goes and what people do with trash once it's thrown away.

Before transitioning to interest areas, invite children to use the computer with adult assistance during choice time to research the question.

Choice Time

As you interact with children in the interest areas, make time to

- Help them use the computer to research where trash goes once it's thrown away.

> **For more information about helping children use the Internet to find answers to their questions, see Intentional Teaching Card LL26, "Searching the Web."**

Read-Aloud

Read *Sam Helps Recycle.*

- **Before you read**, show children the cover of the book. Ask, "What do you think this book will be about?"

- **As you read**, respond to children's questions about the text and pictures. Talk about the meaning of the word *recycle*.

- **After you read**, ask, "Have you ever seen the garbage truck or a recycling truck in your neighborhood? What did it look like? What else did you notice about it?" Tell the children that the book will be available to them on the computer in the Computer area.

Small Group

Option 1: Rhyming Riddles

- Review Intentional Teaching Card LL11, "Rhyming Riddles." Follow the guidance on the card.

Option 2: Rhyming Chart

- Review Intentional Teaching Card LL10, "Rhyming Chart." Follow the guidance on the card.

Mighty Minutes™

- Use Mighty Minutes 72, "My Body Jumps." Follow the guidance on the card.

Large-Group Roundup

- Recall the day's events.

- Invite children to share what they discovered on their Internet search.

- Tell children that a school custodian, or other school worker who handles the trash, will be coming to class tomorrow. Ask, "What do you want to ask our visitor?"

- Record the children's questions.

Day 2   Investigation 2

Where does trash go?
What do workers do there?

Vocabulary

See Book Discussion Card 11, *Radio Man (Don Radio)*, for words.

Large Group

Opening Routine

- Sing a welcome song and talk about who's here.

Movement: The Kids Go Marching In

- Use Mighty Minutes 70, "The Kids Go Marching In." Follow the guidance on the card.

Discussion and Shared Writing: Follow That Trash

- Review the question of the day.

- Introduce the school custodian, or other school worker, who handles the trash.

- Invite the children to ask the questions they thought of in yesterday's large-group roundup.

- Ask your guest, "When we throw something away, where does it go when it leaves our classroom?"

- Record his or her explanation.

- Ask the visitor, "May we follow you to watch what you do with the trash?"

- Use a map of the school, or create your own map, to trace the path the visitor takes when you and the children follow the visitor to dispose of the trash. Mark all the stops that the trash makes along the way, e.g., the trash might first be put in the big trash can outside the kitchen door, and then carried to the dumpster behind the school.

Before transitioning to interest areas, talk about the items that children can take apart in the Discovery area and how children may use them. Loosen any tight screws to make the items easier to disassemble.

Choice Time

As you interact with children in the interest areas, make time to

- Observe how they explore the items in the Discovery area.

- Notice how the children use the tools and what discoveries they make.

> **For more information on setting up and maintaining the Discovery area, see *The Creative Curriculum for Preschool, Volume 2: Interest Areas.***

Read-Aloud

Read *Radio Man*

- Use Book Discussion Card 11, *Radio Man.* Follow the guidance for the second read-aloud.

English-language learners
When observing English-language learners, you may notice that some children repeat English words or phrases quietly to themselves. These children are rehearsing the language—they are figuring out pronunciation, intonation, grammar, and what words mean. They are also practicing new vocabulary.

Small Group

Option 1: How Big Around?

- Review Intentional Teaching Card M62, "How Big Around?" Follow the guidance on the card using items of different sizes from the junk collection.

Option 2: Which Container Holds More?

- Review Intentional Teaching Card M32, "Which Container Holds More?" Follow the guidance on the card.

Mighty Minutes™

- Use Mighty Minutes 47, "Step Up." Follow the guidance on the card, using the chart from yesterday's large-group roundup.

Large-Group Roundup

- Recall the day's events.

- Remind the children of the path that the classroom trash takes on its way out of the school. Ask, "How can we find out what happens to the trash after it leaves our school?"

- Tell children about the sanitation worker who will be visiting the classroom tomorrow.

- Ask, "What would you like to ask our new visitor tomorrow?"

- Record children's questions.

If you can't find a sanitation worker to visit the classroom, check your area's trash collection schedule. Arrange to have the children observe the workers and the truck at trash collection time.

Investigation 2

Where does trash go?
What do workers do there?

Vocabulary

English: *real, pretend*

Spanish: *real, imaginario*

Large Group

Opening Routine

- Sing a welcome song and talk about who's here.

Song: "Recycle Song"

- Use Mighty Minutes 71, "Recycle Song." Follow the guidance on the card.

> Remember to take photos of the children interviewing the visitor. Display the photos with the children's questions to document learning throughout the study.

Discussion and Shared Writing: Expert Interview

- Introduce the sanitation worker.

- Ask the visitor to explain what he or she does at work.

- Invite the children to ask their questions from yesterday's large-group roundup.

- Record the visitor's responses.

Before transitioning to interest areas, talk about the toy garbage trucks in the Block area and how children may use them.

Choice Time

As you interact with children in the interest areas, make time to

- Observe children as they play with the garbage trucks.

- Pay attention to how the children use what they've learned during the study in their play.

Read-Aloud

Read *Sam Helps Recycle.*

- **Before you read**, say, "We've learned a lot from interviewing experts. Let's read this book again and see if Sam's trash gets moved around like ours does."

- **As you read**, pause and relate information in the book to information that the visitors have shared.

- **After you read**, make a list of all of the recyclable items in the story. Save the list for tomorrow's large-group discussion. Tell the children that the book will be available to them on the computer in the Computer area.

Small Group

Option 1: Bookmaking

- Review Intentional Teaching Card LL04, "Bookmaking."

- Say, "We know a lot about the real places that our trash goes." Recall with children the interviews with the school custodian and the sanitation worker.

- Invite children to think of imaginary places that trash might go. Say, "Let's make a book about all of the *pretend* places that our trash might go."

- Follow the guidance on the card to help the children create a book.

Option 2: Desktop Publishing

- Review Intentional Teaching Card LL02, "Desktop Publishing."

- Say, "We know a lot about the real places that our trash goes." Recall with children the interviews with the school custodian and the sanitation worker.

- Invite children to think of imaginary places that trash might go. Say, "Let's make a book about all of the *pretend* places that our trash might go."

- Follow the guidance on the card to help the children create a book on the computer.

> As children develop, the difference between reality and make-believe gradually becomes clearer. While preschool children generally know the difference between what is real and what is pretend, they sometimes get confused and think that what they imagined is real.

Mighty Minutes™

- Use Mighty Minutes 38, "Spatial Patterns." Follow the guidance on the card.

Large-Group Roundup

- Recall the day's events.

- Write a group thank-you note to the school custodian and another to the visiting sanitation worker. Invite the children to add drawings to the note and sign their names.

Day 4 Investigation 2

Where does trash go?
What do workers do there?

Vocabulary

English: *crush*

Spanish: *aplastar*

See Book Discussion Card 11, *Radio Man* (*Don Radio*), for additional words.

Large Group

Opening Routine

- Sing a welcome song and talk about who's here.

Song: "Recycle Song"

- Use Mighty Minutes 71, "Recycle Song." Follow the guidance on the card.

Discussion and Shared Writing: Dump or Recycle?

- Review with the children what happens in *Sam Helps Recycle*.

- Relate the story to what they learned through their interviews with the custodian and the sanitation worker.

- Provide a collection of safe trash items for the children to sort.

- Say, "I have a bunch of mixed-up trash. I need help sorting it. Some things can be thrown away and some can be recycled."

- Invite the children to sort the trash.

- As they sort, refer to the list of items from yesterday's book discussion that can be recycled. Add items to the list as necessary. Point out the recycling symbol on some of the items.

- Explain that children may start recycling items that are used in the classroom.

- Ask, "What things in the classroom can be recycled?"

- Record children's responses.

- Say, "I need some help deciding where we should put the recycling boxes." Invite children to choose the best places for collecting recyclable items.

Before transitioning to interest areas, review the question of the day. Talk about the cans and the can crusher in the Discovery area and explain how the children may use them.

Choice Time

As you interact with children in the interest areas, make time to

- Invite children to find out how many uncrushed cans will fit in a small trash can. Have the children compare that number with the number of *crushed* cans that will fit in the same trash can.

- Relate the experience of crushing cans to the trash getting crushed in the back of a garbage truck.

Read-Aloud

Read *Radio Man.*

- Use Book Discussion Card 11, *Radio Man.* Follow the guidance for the third read-aloud.

Small Group

Option 1: Bookmaking

- Review Intentional Teaching Card LL04, "Bookmaking."

- Say, "We know a lot about the real places that our trash goes." Recall with children the interviews with the school custodian and the sanitation worker.

- Invite children to think of imaginary places that trash might go. Say, "Let's make a book about all of the pretend places that our trash might go."

- Follow the guidance on the card to help the children create a book.

Option 2: Desktop Publishing

- Review Intentional Teaching Card LL02, "Desktop Publishing."

- Say, "We know a lot about the real places that our trash goes." Recall with children the interviews with the school custodian and sanitation worker.

- Invite children to think of imaginary places that trash might go. Say, "Let's make a book about all of the pretend places that our trash might go."

- Follow the guidance on the card to help the children create a book on the computer.

> **By helping children imagine the pretend places that trash might go, you are using decontextualized language, or talking about another time or place. This type of talk is important for future reading success because most books are written about other times and places, some of which are imaginary.**

Mighty Minutes™

- Use Mighty Minutes 01, "The People in Your Neighborhood."

- Create new verses using references to custodians or sanitation workers.

Large-Group Roundup

- Recall the day's events.

- Invite children who crushed cans in the Discovery area to share what they learned.

Investigation 3

How do trash and garbage affect our community?

	Day 1	Day 2
Interest Areas	**Blocks:** empty boxes of various sizes	**Art:** paper; markers; paint
Question of the Day	Should you throw paper out the window of a car or building?	Are monsters real or pretend?
Large Group	**Poem:** "The Litter Monster" **Discussion and Shared Writing:** Litter **Materials:** Mighty Minutes 69, "The Litter Monster"; small pile of trash; fan; digital camera	**Poem:** "The Litter Monster" **Discussion and Shared Writing:** Litter and Animals **Materials:** Mighty Minutes 69, "The Litter Monster;" *The Adventures of Gary & Harry*
Read-Aloud	*The Adventures of Gary & Harry* Book Discussion Card 09 (first read-aloud)	*I Stink!*
Small Group	**Option 1: Seek and Find** Intentional Teaching Card M03, "Seek and Find"; junk collection; large basket **Option 2: Sorting and Classifying** Intentional Teaching Card M05, "Sorting & Classifying"; objects that define boundaries for sorting; junk collection	**Option 1: Story Problems** Intentional Teaching Card M22, "Story Problems"; collection of manipulatives **Option 2: Dinnertime** Intentional Teaching Card M01, "Dinnertime"; paper or plastic dishes; utensils; napkins; cups; place mats
Mighty Minutes™	Mighty Minutes 47, "Step Up"	Mighty Minutes 46, "Strolling Through the Park"

Day 3	Make Time For...

Discovery: junk collection

Outdoor Experiences

Physical Fun

- Review Intentional Teaching Card P14, "Moving Through the Forest." Follow the guidance on the card.

Which will we find more of on our litter walk: paper or bottles?

Family Partnerships

- Invite a family member who plays a musical instrument to visit during the next investigation to help the children make instruments.
- Ask family members to contribute old wrapping paper and gift boxes of different sizes. Save these items for Investigation 5, "How can we create less trash?"

Poem: "The Litter Monster"

Discussion and Shared Writing: Litter Walk

Materials: Mighty Minutes 69, "The Litter Monster"; gloves for all the children; junk collection

Wow! Experiences

- Day 3: A litter walk around the school

The Adventures of Gary & Harry
Book Discussion Card 09
(second read-aloud)

Option 1: What's Missing?

Intentional Teaching Card LL18, "What's Missing?"; bag or box with items from the junk collection; large piece of cardboard or paper

Option 2: Memory Games

Intentional Teaching Card LL08, "Memory Games"; memory game, lotto game, or collection of duplicate pictures/objects

Mighty Minutes 85, "Listen for Your Name"

Day 1 | Investigation 3

How do trash and garbage affect our community?

Vocabulary

English: *litter*

Spanish: *basura esparcida*

See Book Discussion Card 09, *The Adventures of Gary & Harry (Las aventuras de Gary y Harry),* for additional words.

Large Group

Opening Routine

• Sing a welcome song and talk about who's here.

Poem: "The Litter Monster"

• Use Mighty Minutes 69, "The Litter Monster." Follow the guidance on the card.

English-language learners
Incorporate gestures as much as possible when reading poems and singing songs.

Discussion and Shared Writing: Litter

• Collect a small pile of trash, and point it out to the children.

• Use a fan to blow the trash around the room.

• Talk about how the little pile of trash is now litter scattered around the classroom.

• Explain, "*Litter* is trash that is not where it belongs. Instead of being in a garbage can or recycling bin, it's on the ground."

• Talk about the question of the day.

• Ask, "Why do we put trash in special places? What do we need to teach the 'litter monster'?"

• Record children's responses.

Before transitioning to interest areas, talk about the empty boxes in the Block area and how children may use them while building.

Choice Time

As you interact with children in the interest areas, make time to

• Observe children as they use the empty boxes in the Block area.

• Ask children questions about what they are doing with the boxes.

• Take pictures of children's constructions and display them in the Block area.

Read-Aloud

- Use Book Discussion Card 09, *The Adventures of Gary & Harry.* Follow the guidance for the first read-aloud.

English-language learners
Before reading a book in English, introduce it to children in their home languages whenever possible. Ask multilingual colleagues or volunteers for help if you don't speak the children's languages.

Small Group

Option 1: Seek & Find

- Review Intentional Teaching Card M03, "Seek & Find." Follow the guidance on the card using the junk collection.

For more information about the components of mathematics, see *The Creative Curriculum for Preschool, Volume 4: Mathematics*, Chapter 1.

Option 2: Sorting & Classifying

- Review Intentional Teaching Card M05, "Sorting & Classifying." Follow the guidance on the card using the junk collection.

Mighty Minutes™

- Use Mighty Minutes 47, "Step Up."

- Try the word variation on the back of the card using the chart you created during large-group time.

Large-Group Roundup

- Recall the day's events.

- Share photos of children's block constructions. Invite children to describe their creations.

Day 2 Investigation 3

How do trash and garbage affect our community?

Vocabulary

English: *litter, incinerator*

Spanish: *basura esparcida, incinerador*

Large Group

Opening Routine

- Sing a welcome song and talk about who's here.

Poem: "The Litter Monster"

- Use Mighty Minutes 69, "The Litter Monster." Follow the guidance on the card.

- Talk about the question of the day.

Discussion and Shared Writing: Litter and Animals

- Show the pages in *The Adventures of Gary & Harry* that talk about Harry's choking on the bag.

- Recall the litter demonstration from yesterday. Ask, "What do you think might happen to animals if there were a lot of *litter* on the ground?" Have children think about the animals in their immediate community.

- Record children's responses.

- Discuss how litter can harm animals. Explain that animals might eat litter and choke; that litter can get in their homes; and that animals can become trapped in litter, which could hurt their bodies.

English-language learners

Whenever possible, make an effort to explain, define, or show children the meaning of the word *litter* and other key vocabulary. This technique helps all children.

Before transitioning to interest areas, talk about the materials in the Art area. Discuss how children may use them to create "Don't be a litter monster" signs for tomorrow's litter walk.

Choice Time

As you interact with children in the interest areas, make time to

- Help children write words on their "Don't be a litter monster" signs.

- Ask them to tell you about any pictures they create for their signs.

Read-Aloud

Read *I Stink!*

- **Before you read**, ask, "What is this book about?"

- **As you read**, talk about the parts of the truck that the book mentions.

- **After you read**, explain how the trash on the barge goes to a big, floating dump or an incinerator. Tell the children that an *incinerator* is "a piece of equipment that burns trash." Explain that an incinerator is like a big fireplace with a door.

Small Group

Option 1: Story Problems

- Review Intentional Teaching Card M22, "Story Problems." Follow the guidance on the card.

Option 2: Dinnertime

- Review Intentional Teaching Card M01, "Dinnertime." Follow the guidance on the card.

Mighty Minutes™

- Use Mighty Minutes 46, "Strolling Through the Park." Follow the guidance on the card.

Large-Group Roundup

- Recall the day's events.

- Invite children who made signs in the Art area to share their work.

Investigation 3

How do trash and garbage affect our community?

Vocabulary

English: *litter*

Spanish: *basura esparcida*

See Book Discussion Card 09, *The Adventures of Gary & Harry (Las aventuras de Gary y Harry)*, for additional words.

Large Group

Opening Routine

- Sing a welcome song and talk about who's here.

Poem: "The Litter Monster"

- Use Mighty Minutes 69, "The Litter Monster." Follow the guidance on the card.

English-language learners
Repeating familiar songs and rhymes with gestures helps English-language learners feel more comfortable participating. It also provides an opportunity for them to practice English.

Discussion and Shared Writing: Litter Walk

- Tell the children that they will be going on a litter walk around the school today.

- Discuss how children can pick up trash safely and remind them that it is important to wear gloves when touching trash.

- Talk about any trash that they shouldn't touch at all, such as broken glass.

- Ask, "What kinds of trash do you think we'll find on our walk today?"

- Talk about the question of the day.

- Record children's responses.

> **Make sure all children wash their hands after returning from the litter walk.**

Before transitioning to interest areas, show an interesting item from the junk collection and describe its shape. Show another item, and ask children to describe its shape. Talk about the junk collection in the Discovery area and how children may sort it by shape.

Choice Time

As you interact with children in the interest areas, make time to

- Talk with children about the shapes they find in the junk collection.

- Invite them to sort objects by shape.

- Help them describe three-dimensional shapes by comparing them to familiar objects, e.g., "This is shaped like a can."

English-language learners
As you discuss each item's shape, show drawings or hold up manipulatives of basic shapes, e.g., circle, square, triangle, or rectangle. Then, as necessary, children can point to the appropriate shapes as they describe their junk during choice time.

Read-Aloud

Read *The Adventures of Gary & Harry.*

- Use Book Discussion Card 09, *The Adventures of Gary & Harry.* Follow the guidance for the second read-aloud.

Small Group

Option 1: What's Missing?

- Review Intentional Teaching Card LL18, "What's Missing?" Follow the guidance on the card using the junk collection.

Option 2: Memory Games

- Review Intentional Teaching Card LL08, "Memory Games." Follow the guidance on the card.

Mighty Minutes™

- Use Mighty Minutes 85, "Listen for Your Name." Follow the guidance on your card.

Large-Group Roundup

- Recall the day's events.

- Invite children to share their experiences from today's litter walk.

Investigation 4

How can we reuse junk?

	Day 1	Day 2	Day 3
Interest Areas	**Art:** items from junk collection **Computer:** eBook version of *Don't Lose It—Reuse It!*	**Music and Movement:** junk collection; variety of containers; wooden blocks	**Art:** art materials for costumes and props; large paper bags
Question of the Day	What can we do with this? (Display an empty paper towel roll.)	Can we use this to make music? (Display a piece of paper.)	Can we use this to make music? (Display potential music maker from the junk collection)
Large Group	**Movement:** Paper Towel Rap **Discussion and Shared Writing:** Amazing Junk **Materials:** Mighty Minutes 64, "Paper Towel Rap"; a paper towel roll for each child; paper bag with items from the junk collection	**Music:** "Musical Junk" **Discussion and Shared Writing:** Instrument Making **Materials:** Mighty Minutes 66, "Musical Junk"; materials for making instruments	**Music:** "Marching Junk Band" **Discussion and Shared Writing:** Preparing to Retell *The Paper Bag Princess* **Materials:** Mighty Minutes 66, "Musical Junk"; materials for making instruments; *The Paper Bag Princess*
Read-Aloud	*Don't Lose It—Reuse It!*	*The Adventures of Gary & Harry* Book Discussion Card 09 (third read-aloud)	*Peter's Chair* Book Discussion Card 10 (first read-aloud)
Small Group	**Option 1: Straw Shapes** Intentional Teaching Card M42, "Straw Shapes"; geometric shapes; drinking straws of varying lengths; paper; pencils or crayons **Option 2: 3-D Shapes** Intentional Teaching Card M42, "Straw Shapes"; clay; paper; pencils or crayons; geometric shapes; drinking straws of varying lengths; nonstandard measuring tools	**Option 1: More or Fewer Towers** Intentional Teaching Card M12, "Measure & Compare"; nonstandard measuring tools **Option 2: Cover Up** Intentional Teaching Card M34, "Cover Up"; masking tape; pictures and samples of various floor coverings; blocks; paper; pencils or crayons	**Option 1: Dramatic Retelling of** *The Paper Bag Princess* Intentional Teaching Card LL06, "Dramatic Story Retelling"; *The Paper Bag Princess*; story props **Option 2: Clothesline Retelling of** *The Paper Bag Princess* Intentional Teaching Card LL33, "Clothesline Storytelling"; *The Paper Bag Princess*; lamination supplies or clear adhesive paper; 6-ft clothesline; clothespins; a paper star; paper; marker; large resealable bag
Mighty Minutes™	Mighty Minutes 57, "Find the Letter Sound"; letter cards	Mighty Minutes 07, "Hippity, Hoppity, How Many?"	Mighty Minutes 15, "Say It, Show It"; container with lid; several small manipulatives

Day 4	Day 5	Make Time For…
Art: paper bags of different sizes	**Art:** some of the junk items described in *Don't Lose It—Reuse It!*; junk collection **Computer:** eBook version of *Don't Lose It—Reuse It!*	## Outdoor Experiences • Fill a couple of big containers with a mix of clean trash and recyclable items. • Place a trash can and a recycling bin several yards away from the containers. • Have children work in small groups to run a trash relay. • In this relay, one child picks out an item from one of the containers and runs across to the trash can and recycling bin. The child drops the item in the appropriate bin and runs back. Then the next child takes a turn. • Take pictures.
Can we make something from this paper bag?	What can we make from this? (Display junk collection item.)	
Song: "Recycle Song" **Discussion and Shared Writing:** Paper Bags **Materials:** Mighty Minutes 71, "Recycle Song"; paper bags of different sizes; junk collection	**Book:** *Don't Lose It—Reuse It!* **Discussion and Shared Writing:** Gift Making **Materials:** *Don't Lose It—Reuse It!*; collection of found objects	## Family Partnerships • Ask families to bring in something from home that they consider trash but could be used to create something useful, e.g., empty plastic mayonnaise jar; cereal box; empty wrapping paper roll. • Continue to ask family members to send in old wrapping paper and gift boxes of varied sizes. Save them for Investigation 5, "How can we create less trash?" • Invite families to access the eBook, *Don't Lose It—Reuse It!*
Hush! A Thai Lullaby	*Peter's Chair* Book Discussion Card 10 (second read-aloud)	
Option 1: Stick Letters Intentional Teaching Card LL28, "Stick Letters"; collection of sticks; alphabet cards **Option 2: Walk a Letter** Intentional Teaching Card LL17, "Walk a Letter"; masking tape; alphabet cards	**Option 1: Dramatic Retelling of *The Paper Bag Princess*** Intentional Teaching Card LL06, "Dramatic Story Retelling"; *The Paper Bag Princess*; story props **Option 2: Clothesline Retelling of *The Paper Bag Princess*** Intentional Teaching Card LL33, "Clothesline Storytelling"; *The Paper Bag Princess*; lamination supplies or clear adhesive paper; 6-ft clothesline; clothespins; a paper star; paper; marker; large resealable bag	## Wow! Experiences • Day 2: A visit from a family member who plays a musical instrument.
Mighty Minutes 16, "Nothing, Nothing, Something"	Mighty Minutes 07, "Hippity, Hoppity, How Many?"	

Day 1 Investigation 4

How can we reuse junk?

Vocabulary

English: *amazing*

Spanish: *asombrosa*

Large Group

Opening Routine

• Sing a welcome song and talk about who's here.

Movement: Paper Towel Rap

• Review the question of the day.

• Use Mighty Minutes 64, "Paper Towel Rap." Follow the guidance on the card.

Discussion and Shared Writing: Amazing Junk

• Fill a paper bag with interesting items from the junk collection to create a mystery bag.

• Have each child select one item from the mystery bag.

• Ask, "Wow! What can we do with this *amazing* junk?"

• Invite children to think of different things they could make.

• Record their responses.

Before transitioning to interest areas, tell the children that they may use the items in the junk collection to make some of the things they just mentioned.

> **Using your facial expressions and tone of voice to convey excitement about study-related events motivates children to continue their investigations of the topic.**

Choice Time

As you interact with children in the interest areas, make time to

• Talk about how parts of broken toys might be used for something new. For example, broken crayons could be melted to create a whole new crayon.

• Help children create a lost-and-found area for toy parts that could be used in a different way.

Read-Aloud

Read *Don't Lose It—Reuse It!*

- **Before you read**, ask, "What do you think this book will be about?"

- **As you read**, pause and invite children to guess what will be made with the objects.

- **After you read**, look back at some of the pictures in the book. Invite children to discuss ideas they would like to try. Tell the children that the book will be available to them on the computer in the Computer area.

Small Group

Option 1: Straw Shapes

- Review Intentional Teaching Card M42, "Straw Shapes." Follow the guidance on the card, using the junk collection.

Option 2: 3-D Shapes

- Review Intentional Teaching Card M42, "Straw Shapes."

- Follow the guidance on the card. Invite children to create three-dimensional shapes using clay.

English-language learners
Teacher-guided small-group activities may make it easier for children who are English-language learners to become involved and interact with others. The small-group structure helps them transition from working in isolation to participating in larger groups.

Mighty Minutes™

- Use Mighty Minutes 57, "Find the Letter Sound." Follow the guidance on the card.

Large-Group Roundup

- Recall the day's events.

- Invite children to share some of the things they made with items from the junk collection.

Day 2 Investigation 4

How can we reuse junk?

Vocabulary

See Book Discussion Card 09, *The Adventures of Gary & Harry (Las aventuras de Gary y Harry)*, for words.

Large Group

Opening Routine

- Sing a welcome song and talk about who's here.

Music: "Musical Junk"

- Review the question of the day.

- Use Mighty Minutes 66, "Musical Junk." Follow the guidance on the card, using the piece of paper displayed for the question of the day.

> **"Musical Junk" is an excellent way to use the arts to teach environmental concepts.**

Discussion and Shared Writing: Instrument Making

- Say, "We made music just by using a piece of paper. Let's see what other things we can use to make instruments."

- Provide a variety of materials that allow the children to experiment with making instruments. These materials could include two wooden blocks or various containers for drumming, or objects children can tap on the floor.

- Invite children to brainstorm different ways to make instruments from the junk collection. Record children's suggestions.

Before transitioning to interest areas, introduce the family volunteer and talk about how the children can use the materials in the Art area to make instruments.

Choice Time

As you interact with children in the interest areas, make time to

- Ask them questions about their process. "Why did you choose the bottle? What will you add next?"

- Invite the family member to share his experiences with musical instruments.

English-language learners

Explaining a process is a higher-level skill that is often one of the most difficult for children to acquire. Children might be able to analyze simple tasks before being able to express their thoughts in English. To help them, explain each of the steps in the process as it is completed. Have frequent, informal conversations with children about what they are doing.

Read-Aloud

Read *The Adventures of Gary & Harry.*

- Use Book Discussion Card 09, *The Adventures of Gary & Harry.* Follow the guidance on the card for the third read-aloud.

Small Group

Option 1: More or Fewer Towers

- Review Intentional Teaching Card M12, "Measure & Compare." Follow the guidance on the card.

Option 2: Cover Up

- Review Intentional Teaching Card M34, "Cover Up." Follow the guidance on the card.

Mighty Minutes™

- Use Mighty Minutes 07, "Hippity, Hoppity, How Many?" Follow the guidance on the card.

- Encourage children to lead the activity.

Large-Group Roundup

- Recall the day's events.
- Review the question of the day.
- Invite children to share the instruments they made in the Art area today.

Day 3 Investigation 4

How can we reuse junk?

Vocabulary

See Book Discussion Card 10,
Peter's Chair (La silla de Pedro), for words.

Large Group

Opening Routine

- Sing a welcome song and talk about who's here.

Music: "Marching Junk Band"

- Review the question of the day.

- Use Mighty Minutes 66, "Musical Junk."

- Invite the children to march around the room playing music with the instruments they made yesterday.

> For more information on how music supports children's development and learning, see *The Creative Curriculum for Preschool, Volume 2: Interest Areas*, Chapter 13.

Discussion and Shared Writing: Preparing to Retell *The Paper Bag Princess*

- Read *The Paper Bag Princess*.

- Explain, "Sometimes we use music to help retell stories. Today, we are going to retell *The Paper Bag Princess* during small-group time. We'll use the instruments we made yesterday to help us tell the story. What else do we need to help us tell the story?"

- Look back through the pages of the book for ideas.

- Invite children to think of some costumes and props that would help them tell the story.

- Record their ideas.

Before transitioning to interest areas, talk about the materials in the Art area. Discuss how the children may use them to create the costumes and props they mentioned earlier.

Choice Time

As you interact with children in the interest areas, make time to

- Talk to the children as they make costumes and props. Ask them about their process.

- Invite them to refer to the list for ideas.

Read-Aloud

Read *Peter's Chair.*

- Use Book Discussion Card 10, *Peter's Chair.* Follow the guidance for the first read-aloud.

Small Group

Option 1: Dramatic Retelling of
The Paper Bag Princess

- Review Intentional Teaching Card LL06, "Dramatic Story Retelling." Follow the guidance on the card to retell *The Paper Bag Princess.*

Option 2: Clothesline Retelling of
The Paper Bag Princess

- Review Intentional Teaching Card LL33, "Clothesline Storytelling." Follow the guidance on the card to retell *The Paper Bag Princess.*

Mighty Minutes™

- Use Mighty Minutes 15, "Say It, Show It." Follow the guidance on the card.

Large-Group Roundup

- Recall the day's events.
- Show photos of the trash can and recycling bin relay game that the children have been playing outdoors.

Investigation 4

How can we reuse junk?

Vocabulary

English: *reused*

Spanish: *reutilizado*

Large Group

Opening Routine

- Sing a welcome song and talk about who's here.

Song: "Recycle Song"

- Use Mighty Minutes 71, "Recycle Song." Follow the guidance on the card.

Discussion and Shared Writing: Paper Bags

- Show a few paper bags of different sizes.

- Review the question of the day.

- Ask, "What are some of the things we can do with a paper bag? How can we *reuse* it?" Listen for children's responses, which might include wrapping presents, making books, making puppets, collecting trash, or making costumes.

- Record the children's responses.

Before transitioning to interest areas, talk about the various paper bags in the Art area. Discuss how children may use them to make or do some of the things they listed during large-group time.

Choice Time

As you interact with children in the interest areas, make time to

- Help children think of different ways to reuse materials, such as drawing on both sides of the paper or building something out of old cardboard boxes.

Read-Aloud

Read *Hush! A Thai Lullaby.*

- **Before you read**, ask, "What is this book about?"

- **As you read**, pause and invite children to fill in the repetitive text.

- **After you read**, talk about the animal sounds. Explain that people who speak other languages say animal sounds differently. For example, "The duck in the book says *ghap, ghap.* When I make a duck sound, I say *quack, quack.*" Invite children to share their own versions of the animal sounds in the story. Talk about their similarities and differences.

Small Group

Option 1: Stick Letters

- Review Intentional Teaching Card LL28, "Stick Letters." Follow the guidance on the card.

Option 2: Walk a Letter

- Review Intentional Teaching Card LL17, "Walk a Letter." Follow the guidance on the card.

These two small-group activities provide a multisensory way of learning that letters are made of straight, curved, and slanted lines. As you draw children's attention to these line segments, you are preparing them for handwriting.

Mighty Minutes™

- Use Mighty Minutes 16, "Nothing, Nothing, Something." Follow the guidance on the card.

Large-Group Roundup

- Recall the day's events.

- Invite children to talk about how they reused the paper bags in the Art area today.

How can we reuse junk?

Vocabulary

See Book Discussion Card 10,
Peter's Chair (La silla de Pedro), for words.

Large Group

Opening Routine

- Sing a welcome song and talk about who's here.

Book: *Don't Lose It—Reuse It!*

- Reread *Don't Lose It—Reuse It!*

- Ask, "Who remembers what the word *reuse* means?"

Discussion and Shared Writing: Gift Making

- Review the question of the day.

- Talk about the interesting things that the children in the book made with found objects.

- Invite children to think about something they would like to make for someone else using items from the junk collection.

- If children need help, pass around a collection of items. As they explore each item, ask, "What could we make with this?" Offer suggestions as needed.

- Record children's ideas.

Before transitioning to interest areas, talk about the variety of materials in the Art area. Discuss how the children can use them to make gifts. Also tell the children that the book *Don't Lose It—Reuse It!* will be available to them on the computer in the Computer area.

Choice Time

As you interact with children in the interest areas, make time to

- Talk to the children about their work in the Art area.

- Encourage them to view objects in new ways. Say, for example, "This metal can had green beans in it. I wonder how we could reuse it to hold something else."

Read-Aloud

Read *Peter's Chair.*

- Use Book Discussion Card 10, *Peter's Chair.* Follow the guidance for the second read-aloud.

Small Group

Option 1: Dramatic Retelling of
The Paper Bag Princess

- Review Intentional Teaching Card LL06, "Dramatic Story Retelling." Follow the guidance on the card to retell *The Paper Bag Princess.*

Option 2: Clothesline Retelling of
The Paper Bag Princess

- Review Intentional Teaching Card LL33, "Clothesline Storytelling." Follow the guidance on the card to retell *The Paper Bag Princess.*

> Repeating story retelling activities is an effective strategy for developing children's comprehension and their understanding of story structure. Retelling activities support the development of many other components of literacy as well.

Mighty Minutes™

- Use Mighty Minutes 07, "Hippity, Hoppity, How Many?" Follow the guidance on the card.

Large-Group Roundup

- Recall the day's events.
- Invite children who made gifts in the Art area to share their creations.

Investigation 5

How can we create less trash?

	Day 1	Day 2
Interest Areas	**Art:** some of the junk items described in *Don't Lose It—Reuse It!;* junk collection	**Dramatic Play:** wrapping paper scraps; tape; scissors; variety of boxes
Question of the Day	What do you do with clothes that don't fit you anymore?	Will this present fit in this box? (Display a present made from the junk collection and a small box.)
Large Group	**Movement:** Let's Stick Together **Discussion and Shared Writing:** Reusing **Materials:** Mighty Minutes 67, "Let's Stick Together"; magnet; article of clothing that you no longer wear; *Sam Helps Recycle*	**Movement:** Silly Willy Walking **Discussion and Shared Writing:** Using Less in the Classroom **Materials:** Mighty Minutes 05, "Silly Willy Walking"; sheets of paper; small trash can
Read-Aloud	*Something From Nothing*	*I Stink!*
Small Group	**Option 1: Guessing Jar** Intentional Teaching Card M17, "Guessing Jar"; large plastic jar; collection of objects to put in jar **Option 2: Which Has More?** Intentional Teaching Card M19, "Which Has More?"; ice cube trays or egg cartons; resealable bags; objects of similar size	**Option 1: I'm Thinking of a Shape** Intentional Teaching Card M20, "I'm Thinking of a Shape"; geometric solids; empty containers shaped like the geometric solids **Option 2: Shape Book** Intentional Teaching Card M20, "I'm Thinking of a Shape"; geometric solids; empty containers shaped like the geometric solids; junk collection; digital camera; materials to make a book
Mighty Minutes™	Mighty Minutes 65, "People Patterns"	Mighty Minutes 25, "Freeze"; dance music; letter cards

Day 3

Dramatic Play: wrapping paper scraps; tape; scissors; variety of boxes

Do you like to eat this? (Display a familiar piece of food packaging with environmental print.)

Music: "The Kids Go Marching In"

Discussion and Shared Writing: So Much Trash

Materials: Mighty Minutes 70, "The Kids Go Marching In"; bag of groceries; shovel; *Sam Helps Recycle*

Peter's Chair
Book Discussion Card 10
(third read-aloud)

Option 1: I Went Shopping

Intentional Teaching Card LL31, "I Went Shopping"; 5–6 pieces of environmental print; grocery bag

Option 2: Shopping Word Wall

Intentional Teaching Card LL31, "I Went Shopping"; 5–6 pieces of environmental print; grocery bag; scissors

Mighty Minutes 72, "My Body Jumps"

Make Time For...

Outdoor Experiences

Physical Fun

- Review Intentional Teaching Card P18, "Dribbling a Ball." Follow the guidance on the card.

Family Partnerships

- Invite family members to share a special snack with the class during the celebration at the end of the study.

How can we create less trash?

Vocabulary

English: *reused*

Spanish: *reutilizado*

Large Group

Opening Routine

- Sing a welcome song and talk about who's here.

Movement: Let's Stick Together

- Use Mighty Minutes 67, "Let's Stick Together." Follow the guidance on the card.

Discussion and Shared Writing: Reusing

- Remind children that Peter's parents in the story, *Peter's Chair*, didn't throw away his old things—instead, they gave them to his sister.

- Show an article of clothing that you don't wear any more. Say, "I was going to throw this away because it doesn't fit me any more."

- Ask, "What could I do with it instead?"

- Review the question of the day.

- Say, "I know I can give someone else my old clothes. And I know from *Peter's Chair* that I can give away furniture that I don't need. I wonder what other things I can give to someone instead of throwing them away. What other things can be *reused* by someone else?"

- Record the children's responses, which might include bikes, toys, games, shoes, or computers.

- Explain, "Just because something isn't useful to us any more doesn't mean that it isn't useful to someone else. When we give something to someone else to use instead of throwing it away, we create less trash."

- Reread the page in *Sam Helps Recycle* that talks about the amount of trash created every day.

English-language learners

Always respond to children when they attempt to communicate, even when their message is unclear. Use the context of the situation to guess what a child means. Respond with a related statement or question. For example, if you think a child is saying *bike*, respond with, "We could give someone else a *bike* to use."

Before transitioning to interest areas, remind children about the materials in the Art area. Discuss how children may use them to make presents. Explain that they will be reusing items from the junk collection, which creates less trash.

Choice Time

As you interact with children in the interest areas, make time to

- Talk with the children about their work. Ask them about their processes.

- Invite them to make cards for their gifts and to do as much writing as possible, including signing their names.

English-language learners
Help children by modeling language for them. Provide language support as you encourage children to interact with each other. For example, say, "Ask Lily, 'May I please have the glue?'"

Read-Aloud

Read *Something From Nothing.*

- **Before you read**, ask, "We read this book earlier in our study. Remember, this book is about a grandfather who makes things from used clothing."

- **As you read**, invite children to tell you what comes next.

- **After you read**, ask, "How did the grandfather reuse the clothing? How many different ways did he reuse it?"

Small Group

Option 1: Guessing Jar

- Review Intentional Teaching Card M17, "Guessing Jar." Follow the guidance on the card.

Option 2: Which Has More?

- Review Intentional Teaching Card M19, "Which Has More?" Follow the guidance on the card.

Mighty Minutes™

- Use Mighty Minutes 65, "People Patterns." Follow the guidance on the card.

Large-Group Roundup

- Recall the day's events.

- Invite children who made gifts or cards in the Art area to share their creations.

How can we create less trash?

Vocabulary

English: *waste, reduce*

Spanish: *desperdiciar, desperdicio, reducir*

Large Group

Opening Routine

- Sing a welcome song and talk about who's here.

Movement: Silly Willy Walking

- Use Mighty Minutes 05, "Silly Willy Walking." Follow the guidance on the card.

Discussion and Shared Writing: Using Less in the Classroom

- Model the act of wasting paper. Write a few words on a piece of paper. Say, "Oops! I made a mistake." Then crumple the paper and throw it into a small trash can. Repeat these steps several times.

- Pay attention to how children respond to your act. If they stop you, stop and discuss the paper you wasted.

- If the children don't stop you, continue your performance until the trash can begins to get full. At that point, stop and notice aloud how wasteful you've been. Say, for example, "Oh no! I used so many sheets of paper! I've almost filled up this whole trash can. I really *wasted* a lot of paper. I've made a lot of trash, and now there isn't as much paper for us to use for drawing and writing later."

- Ask, "What could I have done instead of using so many sheets of paper?"

- Explain, "One way to *reduce,* or create less trash, is to find ways to reuse things that we might throw away, like the items from the junk collection that we're making into presents. Another way to create less trash is to use less. When we use less, we create less trash. That means we don't put as much stuff into the trash can or the recycling bin."

- Ask, "How can we create less trash in our classroom? Can we use less of something?" Prompt children's thinking if necessary by offering examples: "Use only one paper towel instead of two or three. Use less paper in the Art area, and put the caps back on markers so they don't dry out and have to be thrown away."

- Record the children's ideas.

Before transitioning to interest areas, say, "Since we're making presents, it would be nice if we could wrap them." Show the collection of gift boxes and wrapping paper scraps that families have brought in. Explain, "Let's create a store where people can bring their gifts to be wrapped."

Choice Time

As you interact with children in the interest areas, make time to

- Look at the wrapping paper designs together and discuss what occasions the designs represent, e.g., new baby, wedding, holiday, or birthday.

- Help the children create a store where shoppers can bring their gifts to be wrapped. Invite children to take a number, wait their turn, select the paper and the box size, and pay for the gift-wrapping.

- Review the question of the day.

Read-Aloud

Read *I Stink!*

- **Before you read**, ask, "What is the funny name of this book?"

- **As you read**, talk about the items that could have been reused instead of thrown away.

- **After you read**, show the pages that list a piece of trash. Invite children to name other trash and garbage words that they could add to the soup.

Small Group

Option 1: I'm Thinking of a Shape

- Review Intentional Teaching Card M20, "I'm Thinking of a Shape." Follow the guidance on the card.

Option 2: Shape Book

- Review Intentional Teaching Card M20, "I'm Thinking of a Shape." Follow the guidance on the card, using the junk collection.

- Take photos of pieces of junk with different shapes. Invite children to use the photos to create a shape book.

Mighty Minutes™

- Use Mighty Minutes 25, "Freeze." Try the letter sound variation on the back of the card.

Large-Group Roundup

- Recall the day's events.

- Invite children who played in the Dramatic Play area to talk about their experiences at the gift-wrapping store.

Day 3 Investigation 5

How can we create less trash?

Vocabulary

English: *decompose, composting, soil*

Spanish: *degradar, abono orgánico, tierra*

See Book Discussion Card 10, *Peter's Chair (La silla de Pedro)*, for additional words.

Large Group

Opening Routine

- Sing a welcome song and talk about who's here.

Music: "The Kids Go Marching In"

- Use Mighty Minutes 70, "The Kids Go Marching In." Follow the guidance on the card.

Discussion and Shared Writing: So Much Trash

- Bring in a bag of groceries, e.g., cereal box, canned items, items in plastic packaging, and at least one fresh fruit or vegetable.

- Show children the various items in the bag. Talk about the packaging used to keep the food fresh.

- Talk about how much trash is generated from just one bag of groceries.

- Help the children sort out the packaging items that can be recycled. Ask, "Should this packaging go to the dump or a recycling center?"

- Point out how much less trash exists after the recyclables have been set aside.

- Ask, "What about the fresh fruit (or fresh vegetable)? What could we do with the parts that we don't want to eat?"

- Reread the page in *Sam Helps Recycle* where Sam describes how plastic never decomposes.

- Remind children about the apple core, or other piece of organic garbage, that you buried together in the first investigation.

- Take the children outside. Dig up the garbage, and invite the children to look at it.

- Explain, "Food garbage *decomposes*, or breaks apart into tiny pieces and changes in other ways. Some people don't throw their fruit and vegetable scraps in the trash. Instead, they put them in a special container in their yard called a *composting* bin. Every few days, they stir and add yard waste, such as leaves and grass clippings. When the mixture *decomposes*, it becomes soil."

Before transitioning to interest areas, talk about the gift wrap in the Dramatic Play area. Discuss how the children may use it to wrap presents.

Choice Time

As you interact with children in the interest areas, make time to

- Observe children as they wrap presents in the Dramatic Play area.

- Invite them to label the gift-wrap samples and boxes with prices. Offer assistance as necessary.

Read-Aloud

Read *Peter's Chair.*

- Use Book Discussion Card 10, *Peter's Chair.* Follow the guidance on the card for the third read-aloud.

Small Group

Option 1: I Went Shopping

- Review the question of the day.
- Review Intentional Teaching Card LL31, "I Went Shopping." Follow the guidance on the card.

Option 2: Shopping Word Wall

- Review the question of the day.
- Review Intentional Teaching Card LL31, "I Went Shopping." Follow the guidance on the card.
- Cut out words that children recognize on packaging and invite them to add the words to the word wall.

Mighty Minutes™

- Use Mighty Minutes 72, "My Body Jumps." Try the rhyme variation on the back of the card.

Large-Group Roundup

- Recall the day's events.

- Invite children who played in the Dramatic Play area to talk about their experiences in the gift-wrapping store.

Further Questions to Investigate

How can we extend the study further?

If children are still engaged in this study and want to find out more, you might want to investigate additional questions. Here are some suggestions:

- What kinds of trash and garbage are dangerous?

- Is there a place that does not have trash and garbage?

- What happens to old cars and trucks when they no longer run?

- What is the most common kind of trash?

- How do people make recycled paper?

- Why is there so much litter on beaches and in oceans?

Are there additional questions that will help you extend this study?

Our Investigation

Our Investigation

	Day 1	Day 2	Day 3
Interest Areas			
Question of the Day			
Large Group			
Read-Aloud			
Small Group			
Mighty Minutes™			

Day 4	Day 5	Make Time For...
		Outdoor Experiences
		Family Partnerships
		Wow! Experiences

Our Investigation

Vocabulary

English:

Spanish:

Large Group

Choice Time

Read-Aloud

Small Group

Mighty Minutes™

Large-Group
Roundup

Celebrating Learning

Closing the Study

When the study ends—when most of the children's questions have been answered—it is important to reflect and celebrate. Plan a special way to celebrate their learning and accomplishments. Allow children to assume as much responsibility as possible for planning the activities. Here are some suggestions:

- Set up stations in the interest areas for children to show visitors how they investigated reducing, reusing, and recycling.

- Invite families to join the class for a festive Cleanup Day at a local park or recreation area. After picking up trash, have a trash-free picnic.

- Have a Beautiful Junk art show in which everything is made out of found objects.

- Make a class book, photo album, documentation panel, or slide show about the study.

- Set up a "trashketball" game in which the children and their families team up to pitch cans and plastic water bottles into recycling bins.

- Record a video of children demonstrating what they've learned and interviewing each other about reducing, reusing, and recycling. Show the video to the children's families.

- Invite families to an informal Junk Band recital featuring the children playing their junk instruments.

- If possible, time the study to end around April 22 so local Earth Day activities can be part of your closing celebration. Earth Day is always on April 22.

The following pages provide daily plans for two days of celebration. Add your ideas and the children's ideas for how to best celebrate all of their learning.

Celebrating Learning

	Day 1	Day 2	
Interest Areas	**All:** displays of children's investigations. **Computer:** eBook version of *Sam Helps Recycle*	**Dramatic Play:** displays of costumes and props made during the study **Music and Movement:** displays of instruments made during the study	
Question of the Day	What did you like best about the study?	How will you reduce, reuse, and recycle from now on?	
Large Group	**Song:** "Recycle Song" **Discussion and Shared Writing:** Preparing for the Celebration **Materials:** Mighty Minutes 71, "Recycle Song"; junk collection	**Movement:** The Kids Go Marching In **Discussion and Shared Writing:** Interviewing Each Other **Materials:** Mighty Minutes 70, "The Kids Go Marching In"; clipboards; paper; pencils	
Read-Aloud	*Sam Helps Recycle*	*Dinosaur Woods*	
Small Group	**Option 1: Dramatic Retelling of** *Something From Nothing* Intentional Teaching Card LL06, "Dramatic Story Retelling"; *Something From Nothing*; story props **Option 2: Clothesline Retelling of** *Something From Nothing* Intentional Teaching Card LL33, "Clothesline Storytelling"; *Something From Nothing*; lamination supplies or clear adhesive paper; 6 feet of clothesline and clothespins; a paper star; blank paper; marker; large resealable bag	**Option 1: Fruit Salad** Intentional Teaching Card LL35, "Fruit Salad" (See card for equipment, recipe, and ingredients.); musical instruments made from junk **Option 2: Apple Oat Muffins** Intentional Teaching Card M33, "Apple Oat Muffins" (See card for equipment, recipe, and ingredients.); musical instruments made from junk	
Mighty Minutes™	Mighty Minutes 21, "Hully Gully, How Many?"; several items to hold in your hand	Mighty Minutes 69, "The Litter Monster"	

Make Time For...

Outdoor Experiences

Physical Fun

- Review Intentional Teaching Card P18, "Dribbling a Ball." Follow the guidance on the card.

Family Partnerships

- Remind families that they are invited to join the class for a special snack on the second day of the celebration.

Wow! Experiences

- Day 2: Family members visit for the celebration

Day 1　Celebrating Learning

Let's plan our celebration

Vocabulary

English: *celebrate*

Spanish: *celebrar*

Large Group

Opening Routine

- Sing a welcome song and talk about who's here.

Song: "Recycle Song"

- Use Mighty Minutes 71, "Recycle Song." Follow the guidance on the card.

Discussion and Shared Writing: Preparing for the Celebration

- Explain, "We have learned so much about reducing, reusing, and recycling. It's time to *celebrate* all of our hard work!"

- Review the question of the day. Ask, "What would you like to share with our guests about the study at tomorrow's celebration?"

- Record children's responses.

English-language learners
Children who are not yet able to communicate with classmates may feel socially isolated for a time. Inviting families into the classroom so that children can talk with them in their home languages will help children to continue developing social and cognitive skills. Encourage families to find opportunities beyond the classroom for their children to be in social situations in which they can speak their home language.

Before transitioning to interest areas, tell children that you will help them gather the items from the list to create displays for family and friends to see at tomorrow's celebration.

Choice Time

As you interact with children in the interest areas, make time to

- Help children gather the items they would like to share at the celebration.

Read-Aloud

Read *Sam Helps Recycle*.

- **Before you read**, remind children about how much you all have learned from Sam.

- **As you read**, relate the story content to the displays around the room that show children's learning.

- **After you read**, invite children to talk about the part of the study they liked best. Tell the children that the book will be available to them on the computer in the Computer area.

Small Group

Option 1: Dramatic Retelling of *Something From Nothing*

- Review Intentional Teaching Card LL06, "Dramatic Story Retelling." Follow the guidance on the card to retell *Something From Nothing*.

Option 2: Clothesline Retelling of *Something From Nothing*

- Review Intentional Teaching Card LL33, "Clothesline Storytelling." Follow the guidance on the card to retell *Something From Nothing*.

Mighty Minutes™

- Use Mighty Minutes 21, "Hully Gully, How Many?" Follow the guidance on the card.

> When children play this game, they practice verbal number sequence, one-to-one correspondence, and cardinality. (The last number named when counting objects tells how many.) Children must learn these to count as well.

Large-Group Roundup

- Recall the day's events.

- Remind the children of the special celebration tomorrow.

Celebrating Learning

Let's celebrate

Vocabulary

English: *interview, cooperate*

Spanish: *entrevista, cooperar*

Large Group

Opening Routine

- Sing a welcome song and talk about who's here.

Movement: The Kids Go Marching In

- Use Mighty Minutes 70, "The Kids Go Marching In." Follow the guidance on the card.

Discussion and Shared Writing: Interviewing Each Other

- Remind children about the experts they interviewed during the study.

- Ask, "What did we do during those *interviews*?" Help children recall that they asked questions and that you recorded the visitors' answers.

- Explain, "We've learned so much about how we can reduce, reuse, and recycle our trash and garbage. I'm wondering what we all will do differently now that we've learned so much. Let's interview each other and find out."

- Have the children choose a partner and ask, "How will you reduce, reuse, and recycle from now on?"

- Invite families to help children record each other's answers on paper attached to a clipboard.

- After they are finished interviewing each other, invite children to share the answers they recorded.

English-language learners

If you have established a system that pairs English-speaking children with English-language learners, let those children work together to conduct the interviews. If no system exists, help children select their own partners. All children will be successful when they work with partners with whom they feel comfortable.

Before transitioning to interest areas, talk about all of the instruments and costumes that the children made throughout the study. Explain that these things are available in the Music and Movement and the Dramatic Play areas. Discuss how children may use them.

Choice Time

As you interact with children in the interest areas, make time to

- Invite children to talk to family members and other visitors about their work that is displayed around the room.

- Ask children questions that encourage them to recall what they've learned.

Read-Aloud

Read *Dinosaur Woods*.

- **Before you read**, ask, "What do you remember about this book?"

- **As you read**, talk about how the characters might be feeling. Say, "I wonder how the animals feel when they find out that their forest is about to be taken away from them."

- **After you read**, talk about how the animals used teamwork to save the forest. Say, "The animals *cooperated*— worked together—to save their home.

I wonder if they would've succeeded if they hadn't *cooperated*." Ask, "In what ways do we *cooperate* here at school to get things done? "

> **For more information about discussing how characters feel in the stories you read, see Intentional Teaching Card SE05, "Character Feelings."**

Small Group

Option 1: Fruit Salad

- Review Intentional Teaching Card LL35, "Fruit Salad." Follow the guidance on the card.

- While preparing the fruit salad, talk about which packaging and food scraps can be recycled, reused, or composted.

- Share the special snack with family members. As they eat, invite children to recall the study with families and talk about the discoveries that they liked best. Afterward, invite family members to play music together using the children's junk instruments.

Option 2: Apple Oat Muffins

- Review Intentional Teaching Card M33, "Apple Oat Muffins." Follow the guidance on the card.

- While preparing the apple oat muffins, talk about which packaging and food scraps can be recycled, reused, or composted.

- Share the special snack with family members. As they eat, invite children to recall the study and talk about their favorite discoveries. Afterward, invite family members to play music together using the children's junk instruments.

Mighty Minutes™

- Use Mighty Minutes 69, "The Litter Monster."

- Chant or rap the poem and invite children to create a monster dance.

Large-Group Roundup

- Recall the day's events.

- Review the question of the day.

- Write a group thank-you note to the guests for attending the celebration. Post the note in the classroom.

Reflecting on the Study

What were the most engaging parts of the study?

Are there other topics that might be worth investigating?

If I were to change any part of the study, it would be:

Other thoughts and ideas I have:

Resources

Background Information for Teachers

Every living organism produces waste of some kind. *Waste* is matter that no longer has any immediate use—something that is discarded because it lacks value. The waste that humans produce—whether food or nonfood—has a tangible impact on the environment. Given the sheer quantity of waste, it is worthwhile for children to gain some understanding of what kinds of things we discard and what happens to those things after they are thrown away.

Although some people refer to food waste as *garbage* and other waste as *trash*, we tend to use the two words interchangeably. People who study waste, or deal with it professionally, often use the term *municipal solid waste* to describe all trash and garbage that comes from homes, businesses, and schools. Here are other terms related to waste:

dump: an accumulation of discarded items

landfill: burying trash in layers, often involving thick plastic liners to trap harmful seepage; also called a *sanitary landfill*

incinerator: a place where trash is burned, often to produce electricity

biodegradable: a category of garbage that rots or decomposes

compost: fertilizer made from decomposed biodegradable garbage

infectious waste: trash from hospitals, other health care facilities, individuals, and animals that must be contained in special bags and containers because it may cause disease

hazardous waste: materials that are dangerous because they are poisonous, corrosive, explosive, flammable, or radioactive

Disposing of garbage is not a new problem. In fact, humans have been wrestling with it for thousands of years.[1]

- The first city dump opened in Athens, Greece, in 500 B.C.

- The first recycled paper was made in Philadelphia in 1690.

- The first major aluminum recycling plant opened in the United States in 1904.

Trash and garbage have become a serious problem in many countries. Consider, for example, the United States. Although Americans make up only 5% of the world's population, they consume about 30% of the world's resources and thus produce enormous amounts of trash and garbage. In 2007, Americans generated about 254 million tons of waste, or about 4.6 pounds per person per day.[2] This quantity would fill a line of garbage trucks that would stretch about 145,000 miles—more than halfway to the moon! The good news is that Americans recycle and compost 85 million tons of this material, or 1.5 pounds per person per day.[3]

> **What do you want to research to help you understand this topic?**

1. U.S. Department of Energy, Energy Information Administration. (2006). *A primer on solid waste*. Retrieved August 4, 2009, from www.eia.doe.gov/kids/energyfacts/saving/index.html

2. United States Environmental Protection Agency. (2008). *Municipal solid waste generation, recycling, and disposal in the United States: Facts and figures for 2007*. Retrieved August 4, 2009, from www.eia.doe.gov/kids/energyfacts/saving/index.html

3. Ibid., p. 1.

Children's Books

In addition to the children's books specifically used in this *Teaching Guide*, you may wish to supplement daily activities and interest areas with some of the listed children's books.

Adiós, Tricycle (Susan Middleton Elya)

The Adventures of a Plastic Bottle: A Story About Recycling (Alison Inches)

A Box Can Be Many Things (Dana Meachen Rau)

The Crab Man/El hombre de los cangrejos (Patricia E. Van West)

The Dumpster Diver (Janet S. Wong)

The Earth & I (Frank Asch)

Garbage (Robert Maass)

Garbage and Recycling (Rosie Harlow)

Garbage Collectors (Paulette Bourgeois)

The Garden of Happiness (Erika Tamar)

George Saves the World by Lunchtime (Jo Readman)

Grandma Drove the Garbage Truck (Katie Clark)

The Great Paper Caper (Oliver Jeffers)

The Great Trash Bash (Loreen Leedy)

Gullywasher Gulch (Marianne Mitchell)

I Can Save the Earth! One Little Monster Learns to Reduce, Reuse, and Recycle (Alison Inches)

The Keeping Quilt (Patricia Polacco)

My Bag and Me (Karen Farmer)

Not a Box; Not a Stick (Antoinette Portis)

The Paper Bag Prince (Colin Thompson)

The Pink Refrigerator (Tim Egan)

Recycle Every Day (Nancy Elizabeth Wallace)

Recycle! A Handbook for Kids (Gail Gibbons)

Regards to the Man in the Moon (Ezra Jack Keats)

Ten Things I Can Do to Help My World (Melanie Walsh)

The Three R's: Reduce, Reuse, Recycle (Nuria Roca)

Trashy Town (Andrea Zimmerman)

The Wartville Wizard (Don Madden)

Why Should I Recycle? (Jen Green)

Teacher Resources

The teacher resources provide additional information and ideas for enhancing and extending the study topic.

Beautiful Junk: Creative Classroom Uses for Recyclable Materials (Karen Brackett)

Beautiful Stuff! Learning With Found Materials (Cathy Weisman Topal and Lella Gandini)

Ecoart! Earth-Friendly Art & Craft Experiences for 3- to 9-Year-Olds (Laurie Carlson)

Good Earth Art: Environmental Art for Kids (Mary Ann Kohl)

The New 50 Simple Things Kids Can Do to Save the Earth (The Earth Works Group and Sophie Javna)

Waste Not: Time to Recycle (Rebecca Weber)

Weekly Planning Form

Week of: _____   Teacher: _____   Study: _____

	Monday	Tuesday	Wednesday	Thursday	Friday
Interest Areas					
Large Group					
Read-Aloud					
Small Group					

Outdoor Experiences:

Family Partnerships:

Wow! Experiences:

Weekly Planning Form, continued

"To Do" List:

Reflecting on the week:

Individual Child Planning